Also by *The Harvard Lampoon*

Bored of the Rings
Nightlight
The Hunger Pains
The Wobbit

The Best of the
HARVARD
LAMPOON

140 YEARS *of*
AMERICAN HUMOR

THE HARVARD LAMPOON

TOUCHSTONE

New York   London   Toronto   Sydney   New Delhi

Touchstone
An Imprint of Simon & Schuster, Inc.
1230 Avenue of the Americas
New York, NY 10020

First Touchstone hardcover edition November 2016

TOUCHSTONE and colophon are registered trademarks of Simon & Schuster, Inc.

For information about special discounts for bulk purchases,
please contact Simon & Schuster Special Sales at 1-866-506-1949
or business@simonandschuster.com.

The Simon & Schuster Speakers Bureau can bring authors to your live event.
For more information or to book an event, contact the Simon & Schuster Speakers Bureau
at 866-248-3049 or visit our website at www.simonspeakers.com.

Interior design by Erich Hobbing

Manufactured in the United States of America

1   3   5   7   9   10   8   6   4   2

Library of Congress Cataloging-in-Publication Data is available.

ISBN 978-1-5011-0985-0
ISBN 978-1-5011-0989-8 (ebook)

Contents

Introduction

by Simon Rich, Class of 2007

Being chosen to write this introduction is a tremendous honor and I'm humbled that, out of all of the *Harvard Lampoon*'s illustrious alumni, the editors chose to entrust this great task to Conan O'Brien. And when Conan was too busy, B. J. Novak. And when B. J. couldn't do it, Andy Borowitz, and then right on down the line, until they ran out of famous people and things started to get a little desperate, which led to some discussion of "no intro," and then a frantic wiki check to confirm that John Updike was dead, and then a debate about whether or not it would be in bad taste to write something as "Zombie John Updike," and then a brief phone call with the estate of John Updike, and then a handwritten apology note to Updike's adult sons, and then, this morning, a text to me.

The *Harvard Lampoon* was founded in 1876 by seven plucky Harvard undergraduates. And although their first issues now seem somewhat "dated," it's clear that those young racists had a lot of passion about comedy and also other things. Since those early days, the *Harvard Lampoon* has published its magazine continuously. Not even the Vietnam draft could distract the able-bodied, perfectly fit men of the *Lampoon* from writing their wonderful jokes.

The biggest sea change in the *Lampoon*'s history, aside from its decision to let in Irish people, was its shift to television writing. Since the 1970s, *Lampoon* alumni have written for dozens of popular shows, including *SNL*, *Late Night with David Letterman*, *The Simpsons*, *Seinfeld*, *Friends*, *30 Rock*, *The Office*, *Parks and Recreation*, *Girls*, *The Mindy Project*, *Futurama*, and many bad ones, which we don't bring up. It's a remarkable success story. How did a bunch of ragtag, underdog Harvard graduates manage to "make it in America"? Our secret is a little something we call "grit." While other Harvard students are idling away their college days, taking premed classes or exposing war crimes, *Lampoon* editors are hard at work watching reruns of *Mr. Show with Bob and David* or *Kids in the Hall* and then trying to copy those shows but not in a way that's obvious. Like, if a sketch takes place at a restaurant, for example, we would set our piece at a bar, so someone reading the magazine couldn't say we copied *Mr. Show*, because the *Mr. Show* thing was at a restaurant and our thing was at a bar and those are two totally different places. What I'm trying to say is: the story of the *Harvard Lampoon* is the story of America itself.

I've been told that 100 percent of the *Harvard Lampoon's* profits from this book will go toward the already large endowment of the *Harvard Lampoon*. You're probably asking yourself: Aren't there more important causes than an Ivy League comedy magazine? Shouldn't I be buying a book that benefits the poor, the sick, the hungry? How will I be able to sleep at night, knowing that my money has gone to a bunch of privileged teenagers who spend their days drunk inside a castle? If there is a God, how can I look him in the face when I die? How can I stand there, before my maker, be he Jehovah or Allah, and say, "Behold, this is who I am? These are the choices I have made."

The Best of the

HARVARD
LAMPOON

A Plea for Subscribers

1886

The Harvard Lampoon.

Cambridge, October 15, 1886.

Published by-weekly by the Students of Harvard University. Subscription per year (2 vols., 20 nos.), $3.00. Single copies, 20 cents. Address all communications to Harvard Lampoon, Cambridge, Mass.
On sale at Parker House, Young's Hotel, Adams' House, Hotel Brunswick, Hotel Vendome, Lorings', Cupples, Upham & Co., Bowdoin Sq. News Stand, Amee's, Sever's, Co-operative Store. Also at Brentano Bros., New York, Beers & Rankin, New Haven, ——, Princeton.
Subscription payments may be made at the Co-operative Store, or sent to the above address. Contributions and communications may be dropped in the Lampoon box at Foster's Cigar Store.

Present Board of Editors.

L. HONORÉ, '88, *President.*

F. GROVER, '88, *Manager Art Dep't.*

B. W. PALMER, '88, *Secretary and Treasurer.*

WM. ATKINSON, '89. W. H. RAND JR., '88.
R. H. FULLER, '88. O. PRESCOTT JR., '89.
F. L. H. NOBLE.

Business Editors.

G. H. LENT, '88. T. WOODBURY, '89.

THE *Lampoon* Board for this volume will consist of the gentlemen named above. It will be seen that the number of editors is very small; so small, indeed, that it is a great strain upon each individual.

We would like to have about six new men in the art department and six in the literary department, and we hope to receive many contributions, from which we can select new editors or at least have material enough to prevent our labor from becoming too great a task. Pictures (without regard to jokes) and literary contributions should be left in the box at Foster's.

Once more the wheels of the great mill have begun to grind. The grinds have already begun to scan the bulletin boards for announcements regarding the semi-annuals and the giddy society man begins to feel *ennui* resulting from the rule regarding continuous residence. Lampy rouses himself with a yawn and a stretch from his summer lethargy. Quick Kellner! ein glass bier. We have a bad taste in our mouth left over from the second and third of July.

Mechanically we feel in waistcoat pocket for a stray quarter. Not a cent! What's to be done? Why let loose the dogs of subscription. Now look at '90! There's a fine class for you! Unquestionably the best that ever entered College. Come '90, step up and subscribe.

In consideration of the fine intellects that have come among us this year, and consequently the increased faculties for seeing jokes, however weak, we have reduced the price of the *Lampoon* to $3.00 for the entire year. Gentlemanly agents will pass around from building to building and collect the autographs of '90. Don't fail to have your autograph filed in the *Lampoon* office.

Amid the general wreckage of our athletic aspirations last year the success of the class of '89 shone forth as a beacon on the shore we all wished to reach. They kept the Yale Freshman off the fence as regards base ball and as regards boating they went on their way rejoicing, leaving their Yale rivals some six feet under the Thames. We understand, however, that these latter gentlemen ultimately reached the surface, and having discharged several gallons of salt water, sputtered out their congratulations to each other upon having practically won a race which, however, owing to the slight technicality of their not being in at the finish was given to Harvard.

In consideration of this circumstance and also the fact that the "if" prophets at Yale were unanimous in prophesying that Yale "would have won the race" we must advise '89 not to get too "cocky." We must needs take the words of these prophets, inasmuch as

A Cover from 1899

Cover by Paul Bartlett

Worst Aid to the Injured

by Hartwell Bishop and W. Tuckerman (1903)

Send for the Medical Adviser if there is no hope of recovery. Otherwise, proceed as follows:

Hemorrhage. If the flood of blood is bloody, bind a sandwich lightly over bleeding orifice. Insert the point of a fountain pen and twist around until blood bleeds blue.

Jag. Smash windows. Chase away crowd. If there is no crowd to chase away, send for one. Don't waste time going for water; this only irritates the patient. Lay patient flat, and slide down the stairs two or three times. Give stimulant. Keep near the floor. Immerse in water hot as can be borne, or shower with ice water. Rub dry, put in a warm place to cool, and leave for two or three days.

Sprains. Don't breathe while in the room. Get some trustworthy person to hold your breath. One can hold it a minute. After that, get another. Wrap snugly in a rug. Cover with wet woollen cloth. If patient is too obstreperous, let him fix his sprain himself. This will be an excellent drill in self-control for him.

Gas. Send for any debater. They are authorities on this subject.

Fire. If you see a person smoking, do not waste time going for water, but wrap him up in a handkerchief and pour on whiskey or kerosene. A book agent can be put out in a similar manner. If obliged to go through U. 4 in case of fire, lie flatly and go out before it is necessary.

Medical Visitation

Students unable to go out will please report personally the night before. Otherwise as soon as possible.

Remember

Yellow fever, cholera, bubonic plague, and smallpox require attention, and should be reported within two weeks. Otherwise strong complications may result.

The Visitor

A Cover from 1904

Cover by Philip H. Muir

The Breakfast Food Boy

by D. H. Mitchell (1905)

A SWEET and smiling cherub face,
   By name—John Peter Ladle—
Had come to fill an empty place
Within a cushioned cradle.
      His mother called him "darling boy";
      He was his father's midnight joy.

When he had reached the clutching age,
   And pulled his Pa's Imperial,
He had a most abnormal rage
   For predigested cereal.
      Grass, Grape-Nuts, Force, and Maple Flake,
      And all such brain-foods he would take.

So he on nothing else was fed,
   But brain-foods predigested.
His mind grew faster than his head,
   And bumps on it congested.
      (His mother, when she saw the bumps,
      Predicted "bad cerebral mumps.")

The doctor ordered bread and meat,
   And sponge-baths alcoholic;
When Pete proceeded these to eat,
   He quickly had the colic.
      Poor boy! His predigestive diet
      Had so long left his stomach quiet;

His end was sad. He soon returned
   Unto his brain-food diet.
Minus a stomach, he had learned
   That common foods ran riot.
      Faster and faster grew his mind;
      It burst his head, and unconfined,
         Upon the floor ran riot.

The Sport Graceful

by Gluyas Williams (1911)

Aeroplane Comix

by Gluyas Williams (1911)

CATHCART: I'm getting tired of my aeroplane.
DOLOMONDLEY: I knew you'd run it into the ground.

Debutante Comix

by Gluyas Williams (1911)

DÉBUTANTE — You are the first Freshman I've danced with this evening, Mr. Randolph.
YOUNG RANDOLPH— Ee—uh—really? Why, what is there about you for Freshmen to avoid?

The Yearning Point

by Frederick L. Allen (1912)

The Yearning Point

A STORY OF LOVE AND ABSOLUTELY NOTHING ELSE

By Robert W. Sameness

Author of Unknown Raw, etc.

Illustrated by Dunster-Dana-Drayton

SYNOPSIS: Jim Edgeless, a fascinating and well-dressed but penniless and useless aristocrat, has fallen in love successively with Coquette, Mrs. Amiss, Sliquette, and Tiara. Tiara is deeply entranced in turn by four millionaires who are even more useless than Jim; but all this time there is really nobody but Jim. Any girl will explain how this is done. Sliquette loves young Pivott and one or two others. Mrs. Amiss loves anybody she can get her hands on. They are all on an endless house party, and do nothing but drink too much, gamble too much, write love letters to each other, and make love too much. This has been going on a long time. Nothing particular has happened yet, however.

CHAPTER X

CLOACA MAXIMA

The hunting season arrived, and found Tiara curled up in a corner of the scented window seat, looking out over the delicious lawns at the naked trees. She was clad in the laciest of flimsy, intimate silk; thinking, dreaming, now dead, now alive, lips aquiver, the hot tears singeing her throat, and only the rhythmic beating of her pulse broke the silence. She was lonely.

Suddenly a footfall soothed the rug. Instantly she heard it, soft ears tingling.

"Jim!"

He paid no heed. He was looking out over the delicious lawns at the naked trees, watching Miss Pivott, Mrs. Amiss, and Sliquette, who had laid aside their smoking and drinking for the moment to wander over the expensive turf. And as he stood there, flush after flush swept his face. He loved them all, but he was perfectly useless—and he knew it.

"Well?"

He turned a pulsing face to hers. They kissed. It was only natural—the vague inspiration of the moment. Jim managed to force his aching voice out of his scented throat.

"What—is that to me?" he said.

"Nothing," she replied. "I am employed by your father."

Chaos rushed up and down in his forehead.

"You—" he paused.

She quivered. All the intimate, flimsy things quivered diaphanously. Suddenly, a clock ticked. Dreamlike, Tiara waited. It seemed years before he went on, eyes straining, heart thundering.

"You—are adorable!"

Words rushed to her lips. She raised a snowy finger and pushed them back.

"I wonder," she said, after a long time, "why we use such short sentences—when we talk."

He crushed her in his arms. She understood, that was all. The carpet in this room was very expensive.

"Dearest,—I suppose it's because we're both absolutely useless, because we're just like everybody in all the other books—and, perhaps"—he crushed her again—it was deliriously delightful—"perhaps it is because we are paid by the inch."

Kite Comix

by Samuel Otis (1914)

A Cover from 1915

Cover by R. S. Gordon

A Call for Subscribers in
the Form of an Announcement

(1917)

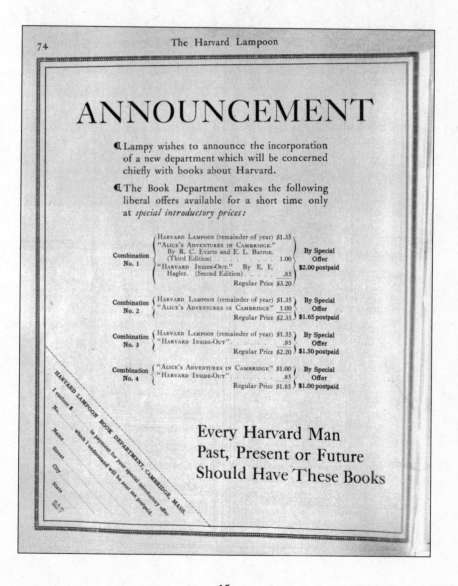

ANNOUNCEMENT

❦ Lampy wishes to announce the incorporation of a new department which will be concerned chiefly with books about Harvard.

❦ The Book Department makes the following liberal offers available for a short time only at *special introductory prices:*

Combination
No. 1

Harvard Lampoon (remainder of year) $1.35
"Alice's Adventures in Cambridge."
By R. C. Evarts and E. L. Barron.
(Third Edition) 1.00
"Harvard Inside-Out." By E. E.
Hagler. (Second Edition) 85
Regular Price $3.20

By Special Offer $2.00 postpaid

Combination
No. 2

Harvard Lampoon (remainder of year) $1.35
"Alice's Adventures in Cambridge" 1.00
Regular Price $2.35

By Special Offer $1.65 postpaid

Combination
No. 3

Harvard Lampoon (remainder of year) $1.35
"Harvard Inside-Out". 85
Regular Price $2.20

By Special Offer $1.50 postpaid

Combination
No. 4

"Alice's Adventures in Cambridge" $1.00
"Harvard Inside-Out". 85
Regular Price $1.85

By Special Offer $1.00 postpaid

HARVARD LAMPOON BOOK DEPARTMENT, CAMBRIDGE, MASS.

I enclose $

No.

Name

Street

City

State

U.S.A.

in payment for your special introductory offer which I understand will be sent me postpaid.

Every Harvard Man
Past, Present or Future
Should Have These Books

A Cover from 1922

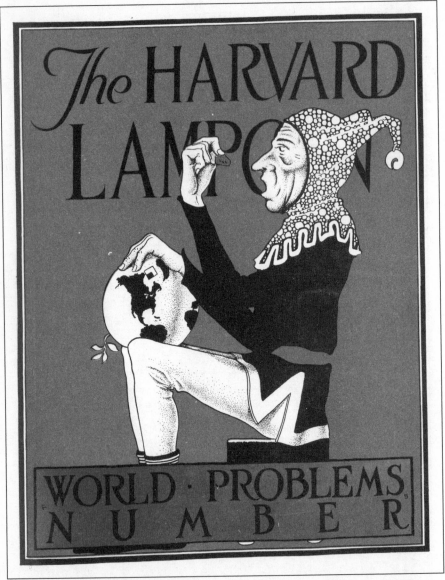

Cover by Francis W. Saunders

The Diary of an Amoeba

by Eugene Reynal (1924)

Jan. 1, 40000000004 BC. This day doth mark an important epoch in mine own development and in that of the earth; inasmuch as at an early hour was I divided from my mother (or was it my father?) and at a still earlier one was the New Year divided from the old. Balance of the morn spent in growing until noon, by which time sufficient size was achieved to enable me to go about wishing the happiness of the season. The Lord only knoweth whence came this custom, as all were so busy dividing that nobody stopped to listen. After a hearty meal did myself commence dividing, which doth seem the vogue. Would that such premium were not placed on following the crowd even in this period of the world, which seemeth near the first. Much tired by my experiences, did strike the timothy early.

Jan. 2. O Lord! Did awake this morn with a splitting headache, and after a light breakfast devoted myself to contemplation and division. What a change hath been wrought overnight, for verily did I retire in the country and upon arising did find a busy town encircling me, with such an array of people as I never hoped to see. If things run on apace, what will come of the world a few years hence? Such thoughts seem but idle musings; for how the world can last so long appeareth beyond the conception of an amoeba. A general undercurrent of excitement passeth among the people, for it is rumored that the ocean subsideth. Some already discourse on

17

leaving these waters and trying to live above it, but this seemeth foolish. As I always sayeth to my last half, "If one is reared in one condition of life, why should he strive to adapt himself to another?"

Jan. 3. This morn doth find the world in terrible state, in that the crowds of yesterday do seem like naught compared to those this day. Immigration laws were passed in greatest haste, but methinks such means ineffective and but the work of politicians, who seemingly do act more from motives inspired to tickle the whims of their constituents than by those in the interest of the common weal. Methinks 'twould be far wiser to elect Amoebess Sanger to the presidency than to give ourselves into the hands of Congressmen who do naught but make mockery of our government. The Lord knoweth it is not for me to talk, whose descendants have already founded and overfilled four towns.

A Call for Subscribers

(1924)

"Oh, Maggie, I Got the Raise!

Here's an extra $50. They've tripled my salary, dear. At twenty-seven I earn $100,000 a year! Home study has made me independent! I am my own boss now. We can live the way we want to live, because I don't envy success, I am it!

"Since birth I've been plugging away at the same old job. I had got in a rut. Then one day I met Calvin C——, who started out with me. He is now president of forty-eight concerns. He said, 'You didn't cut out that coupon, did you?' I said, 'No.' He said, 'Do it now.' So I cut the coupon and I received a year's subscription to the HARVARD LAMPOON for only $3.

"Well, yesterday, the boss was passing my desk. He'd never noticed me before, but when he saw my LAMPOON he rushed over to my desk, grasped my hand, and said, 'Any young man who studies the LAMPOON deserves advancement. I've been watching you, young man, and if I had guessed you were working an hour after supper every night, I'd have promoted you sooner.' He made me a partner on the spot. And now, Maggie, we can have that Rolls Royce we've been saving for."

Mail this coupon today

THE KNOCK OF OPPORTUNITY

You *can* be a success

Send for our amazing booklet. Without cost or obligation of any kind, you can decide to subscribe to the HARVARD LAMPOON for one year. Simply fill out coupon and you will be billed for $3. Do it today — now — this minute.

Be an

- ☐ Architect
- ☐ Archimedes
- ☐ Arch-duchess
- ☐ Arch-fiend
- ☐ Archæologist
- ☐ Archimagus

Be a

- ☐ Bearded Lady
- ☐ College Professor
- ☐ Crown Prince
- ☐ Concrete Expert

Be a

- ☐ Coroner
- ☐ Cow Puncher
- ☐ Good Cook
- ☐ High School Graduate
- ☐ Horse Doctor
- ☐ Heroine
- ☐ Linguist Expert
- ☐ Plumber
- ☐ Potentate
- ☐ Snake Charmer
- ☐ Tight-rope Walker
- ☐ Traveling Salesman
- ☐ Traffic Manager

All communications strictly personal

Training did it. It can do it for you, too. We help you. No sticks to this offer. We don't want your money, we are only interested in your welfare. Every mail brings millions of letters from our former pupils. How much longer are you going to neglect it?

Mail this Coupon

Please send the LAMPOON for one year, also bill of $3.

Name..........................

Address........................

....

The Arms Conference: A Fable

by Eugene Reynal (1924)

Mr. and Mrs. Arms were holding a conference. Young Hans had cut his finger. What should be done about it? After many minutes of meditation, Mr. Arms spoke up.

"I believe," he said, quivering with excitement, "we should bandage it first. It seems to be bleeding."

"No," said his wife, "it must be washed before we can touch it."

"But," replied the husband, renowned for his practical turn of mind, "we cannot wash it, for we have not the right kind of soap." So they deliberated for some time and finally went off in a taxi to get the right kind of soap.

When they returned, more argument ensued. "We should have a doctor," said one. "And a nurse," said the other. "And take him to the hospital," cried the first. "He should have an anaesthetic," rejoined the second. So they set about to do all these things.

In the meanwhile, Hans, unmindful of his family's consternation, tied up his finger in his handkerchief and went out again to the back lot to play with the other boys.

Moral: A glass of water in the hand is better than a bucket of milk spilled on the kitchen floor.

A Call for Subscribers

(1924)

A Call for Subscribers

(1924)

The Harvard Lampoon
Announces
A Contest

Conditions:

1. Open to men and women of every race and creed.

2. Residents of the following countries are eligible: United States and dependencies, United Kingdom, including Canada and Australia, Germany, France, Italy, New York, and other foreign countries lying wholly or partly within the hemispheres.

3. Competent men have consented to act as judges. Every contestant will be given due consideration and only the value of the contributions will be considered.

4. All conditions and terms herein set down must be carefully carried out by each contestant.

5. The winners will be notified immediately.

6. Write clearly on one side of paper only, following directions exactly.

7. Use slip at bottom of this page and fill out as directed.

8. Envelopes should be sealed, stamped and mailed to

CONTEST EDITOR,
The Harvard Lampoon, Inc.,
Lampoon Building,
Cambridge, Mass.

9. No contestant will be considered unless he encloses entrance fee of three dollars.

10. The *prize* will consist of a year's subscription to the LAMPOON, including our already famous St. Nicholas number, due March 27.

11. *Every contestant* will receive a year's subscription to the LAMPOON *absolutely free!*

To The Harvard Lampoon, Inc., Contest Editor.
Lampoon Building, Cambridge, Mass.

The word I wish to submit is...............................

I expect to be judged wholly upon the value of my contribution and will abide by the decision of the judges. I expect you to carry out condition 11 on this page.

CONTEST BLANK
(Follow directions carefully)

Name of contestant ....

Address ....
....
....

I AM ENCLOSING MY ENTRANCE FEE OF THREE DOLLARS

22

A Call for Subscribers

(1924)

23

A Call for Subscribers

(1924)

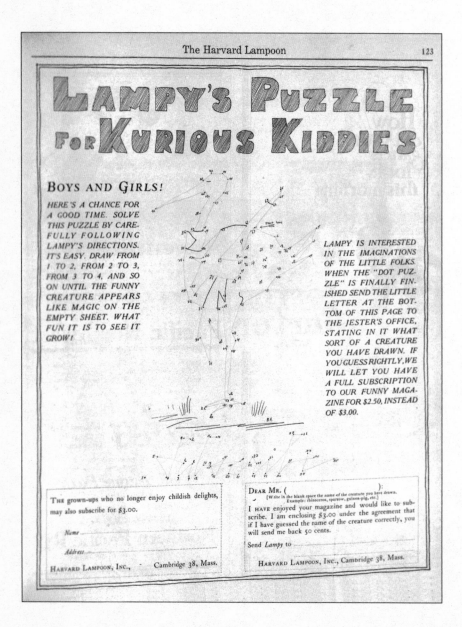

LAMPY'S PUZZLE
FOR KURIOUS KIDDIES

BOYS AND GIRLS!

HERE'S A CHANCE FOR A GOOD TIME. SOLVE THIS PUZZLE BY CARE-FULLY FOLLOWING LAMPY'S DIRECTIONS. IT'S EASY. DRAW FROM 1 TO 2, FROM 2 TO 3, FROM 3 TO 4, AND SO ON UNTIL THE FUNNY CREATURE APPEARS LIKE MAGIC ON THE EMPTY SHEET. WHAT FUN IT IS TO SEE IT GROW!

LAMPY IS INTERESTED IN THE IMAGINATIONS OF THE LITTLE FOLKS. WHEN THE "DOT PUZ-ZLE" IS FINALLY FIN-ISHED SEND THE LITTLE LETTER AT THE BOT-TOM OF THIS PAGE TO THE JESTER'S OFFICE, STATING IN IT WHAT SORT OF A CREATURE YOU HAVE DRAWN. IF YOU GUESS RIGHTLY, WE WILL LET YOU HAVE A FULL SUBSCRIPTION TO OUR FUNNY MAGA-ZINE FOR $2.50, INSTEAD OF $3.00.

THE grown-ups who no longer enjoy childish delights, may also subscribe for $3.00.

Name

Address

HARVARD LAMPOON, INC.,   Cambridge 38, Mass.

DEAR MR. (   ):
[Write in the blank space the name of the creature you have drawn. Example: rhinoceros, sparrow, guinea-pig, etc.]

I HAVE enjoyed your magazine and would like to sub-scribe. I am enclosing $3.00 under the agreement that if I have guessed the name of the creature correctly, you will send me back 50 cents.

Send *Lampy* to

HARVARD LAMPOON, INC., Cambridge 38, Mass.

A Lament

by William W. Scott (1925)

(With sincere apologies to Tennyson)

Broke, broke, broke!
   Yes, cold stony broke. Oh, see
How unpleasant it is to be utter-
   Ly bankrupt and ruined like me!

Oh, well for the janitor's son
   That he troubles not over his suits!
Oh, well for the street cleaner's boy
   That he needs not a shine on his boots!

And bill after bill comes in
   For a larger and larger amount,
And, oh, the "touch" of the firm that is still
   Demanding a sum on account.

Broke, broke, broke!
   For my credit is gone, and I see
That the life of the prodigal spendthrift
   Is wholly unsuited to me.

A Cover from 1934

Cover by Vincent Palmer

12,000 B.C.—The First Practical Joker

by Sidney Carroll (1934)

A Call for Subscribers

(1938)

DON'T BE GLUM <u>ALL</u> THE TIME

Soon, you're going to be getting terribly, terribly, weary. Harvard, you will be finding, is a Serious Place. You will want a ray or two of sunshine. You can ensure a bright and entertaining study table by clipping off the attached coupon and sending it to the *Lampoon* Building, on Mt. Auburn Street. And if you can't find the coupon (our printer is notorious for his absent-mindedness) simply drop in by the side door, deposit $1.50, and with only moderate luck you will receive 12 bright, shiny issues of Harvard's funniest magazine. (Which, with the *Advocate* in the field, is going some.)

LAMPOON $1.50

How I Was Taken at the Cleaners

by Walter R. Bowie, Jr. (1941)

Phenomenal feats of engineering, like why is a strapless bathing suit, have always puzzled me, so maybe my helplessness in coping with the mothproof-bag problem is unique. I think not, however. In fact, I rather suspect that there are many hundreds of thousands who have been buffaloed in a similar way, but dare not admit it, for fear they would look silly. They have something there.

Anyhow, it was this way. In the early summer, an apparently innocent letter from my grandmother came my way. She told me what the weather had been like, and then, with studied carelessness, she slipped in the following casual remark: "I have been wondering about your winter clothes. Moths, as you know, often attack woolens in the summertime, particularly in Cambridge. Go, therefore, to a dry-cleansing establishment and procure a number of mothproof bags, which can be had most reasonably. Your grandfather lost thirty-two dollars at flinch yesterday."

Nothing at all, you see, about how I was expected to get the clothes inside the bags. At the time, I thought of this as a mere oversight, never realizing that my crafty grandmother had no intention of telling me how it was done. For no one in the whole world knows the secret.

But I took her advice, and went down to a dry cleanser's.

"Give me four mothproof bags," I said, slapping down fifty cents on the counter.

The cleanser said nothing, but went into the rear of his shop and came back with the bags.

"How much?" I said.

"Seventy-five cents," he said.

I added a quarter to my fifty cents.

"Apiece," he said.

"I'll take one," I said.

I held up the bag. It was made of paper, and was about ten feet long. The bottom had an open flap, while at the top was a very small hole for the hook of the coat hanger. There were no openings at the sides at all.

"Just moisten that flap at the bottom with saliva," the man said, "after you've got the clothing inside."

"After you've got the clothing inside." Very funny. The man took my seventy-five cents, which was next to the most wretched business deal of the day.

At any rate, I led the bag upstairs to my room, and got ready to put the clothes inside. First I hung a suit neatly on a hanger, emptied all the pockets, and threw moth flakes all over everything. Then I laid the bag across my bed and, holding the suit by the hanger, reached up into the bag as far as I could; but my hand wasn't within four feet of the top of it. I withdrew and looked over the situation. This time, I crawled up inside the bag, dragging the suit with me. After a while, we came to the top, and I pushed the hanger through the little hole. Success seemed certain, but as I turned around in the bag and started back to the open end, my feet tore through the sides, and six bits went up the flue.

I clambered out of the bag, and returned to the cleanser's.

"See here," I said. "You sold me a defective moth bag."

"Did you moisten the flap with saliva?" he said.

"No," I admitted. "Nor did I say 'by the great horn spoon.'"

"Well then," he said. "You'll have to buy a new bag."

He sold me a new bag, which was easily the dirtiest transaction ever.

I went back to my room to start again with different tactics. This

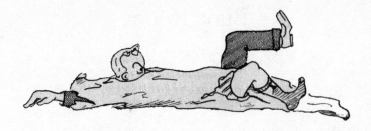

time I stood on the bureau, holding the hanger with one hand, while I tried to drop the bag over the top. This is impossible, and I came about as close as the Phillies. With my grandmother's name and a fearful oath on my lips, I stood there, trembling with rage, when a brilliant thought pierced my consciousness. Quickly I ripped off my clothes, and, taking the suit off its hanger, put it on. Then I pulled the moth bag over my head, and, with the empty hanger in my teeth, began taking off the suit again. In the dark inside the bag I worked feverishly for the better part of an hour and fifteen minutes, but it was no use. I was baffled, licked. Finally, I got panicky, and anybody who thinks I can't fight my way out of a paper bag should have been there. I was terrific. I tore it to small shreds. I mangled it to ribbons. I fell on the bed. I cried.

Buoy Room

by Arthur W. Viner (1942)

I LOVE sailing. Something in my blood, I guess. There are a lot of things in my blood, but this is not the least. Last summer I lived only for the weekly race.

To prepare for the season, I went down to the Cape a week or so early. After looking the old tub over, I scraped it for a few days. This was so much fun, and the weather was so beautiful, that I accidentally scraped a few minor holes in the hull. These were easily fixed by stuffing the *Gazette* in them. Then, on a day when the wind was perfect, I put on my dungarees, and began the real sport of painting the craft. This was marvelous. Bobby Coburn and I had a race to see who would be done first, and if he hadn't broken Right of Way Rule Number 71, I would have won. However, Bobby's infraction caused my boat to crash into a can of paint which he had strategically placed in the way of my foot. It's all in the game, though.

The next week, I was all set for the first race of the season. It was wonderful. We all sat around and argued about it for hours afterward. As usual, Bobby had broken all known rules. Matching our wits against his, we succeeded in forcing him either to accept second place or to have his arm broken. He chose the former, admitting the superiority of our wits over his. This victory was only one of many during the summer. We had many glorious arguments which stimulated our zest for sailing.

What other sport offers the delights of argument, scraping, Bobby Coburn, painting, and relatives? Yes, relatives. After the season had really gotten under way, my four cousins—Benny, Jimmie, and two others—came to visit us. Sailing always attracts a large number of relatives. Mine arrived just in time for the big race. It was another perfect day. Benny and the others went with me as crew and ballast. Ballast is extremely effective where Bobby Coburn is concerned, especially if it has arms and legs. The race was wonderful. We had a contest to see who could get the biggest blisters from not letting go of the mainsheet at the proper time. My cousin Jimmie would have won if Bobby Coburn hadn't stolen the show by dramatically smashing his hand between our boats when he was trying to disqualify us by making us miss the buoy.

After the race, we had fun with another test of skill. We would sail at the pier, and each of us in turn would try to throw the painter over the mooring post while we were still moving. We were happily engaged in this great sport, without interference by Bobby Coburn, because his crew had decided to go swimming, and he was far behind. Our joy didn't last long, though, because Bobby saw our contest and made a beeline for the dock. Wielding his painter furiously, he was just ready to let it go when his boat crashed into the pier, leaving little undamaged except the centerboard, Bobby, and the motor he always used when he was behind.

I'm going down to the Cape tomorrow to have one last sail before it gets too cold. I guess it won't be much fun, though, with nothing to do but putter around in the breeze.

A Call for Subscribers

(1944)

528,900.5 Plumbers in U. S.

More than Three in One – 1,586,701.5 in All – Subscribe for

The Harvard Lampoon

And yet it is *not* a plumbers' journal. They read it for their minds' culture. They need it for its straw votes, its straightforward lack of opinion, its mirror of busy life.

It Saves Their Time

DRUNK & WAGTAILS CO., *Chelsea*   *Lampoon Edition at Newsstands*

Please send the LAMPOON *for one year* **(AT $1.50)** *to*

*(Name)*_____

I leave my tools at

_____

_____

HARVARD LAMPOON

The Terrible Tuba

by George A. Plimpton (1948)

There was only one seat left in the coach that I could see. Throwing my coat on the baggage rack I sat down happily, stretched, grimaced at the inadequacy of leg room on the Pennsylvania Railroad, and opened up a copy of *Coronet*. My seat partner, who had been staring out the train window at the scenery of Boston's South Station, stirred, turned toward me and coughed slightly. I looked up at him. He was a young-looking fellow, still wearing his overcoat and hat and with a nervous twitch in one eye. I smiled the perfunctory smile we keep on hand for seat partners on the Pennsylvania Railroad and returned to my article in *Coronet* on the "World's Smallest Town."

He stirred and coughed again. "I . . . I wonder if you would mind suffering a few indignities," he said.

"Well . . ." I started huffily.

"Hold on, I'm sorry," he interrupted. "That's . . . that's not quite the way I meant to put it." He looked back out the train window again. "I'm afraid I've been under something of a nervous strain," he said, turning back.

"I suppose so," I said slowly.

"Could you take down my name, address, and the time you will spend sitting beside me on this train?" he asked.

The train started with a jolt and the babies couched on mothers' laps began to cry. "I don't see why not," I replied above the din. I wrote down his name and address on the cover of my *Coronet* magazine—Terrence Clark, Harvard U.

I don't think much of college fellows normally, 'count of how I think it's important to work up the hard way like I've done in my business, but this fellow interested me in a way. I asked myself why should he want me to put down his name and address. So when we reached New Haven, I opened the conversation.

35

"College fellow, eh?" I asked.

"I suppose you want to know why I gave you my name, address, and asked you to remember the total time spent with me?" he asked.

"Well now I . . ."

"It's because I think I'm going to be implicated and perhaps framed in a crime of hideous nature," he continued. "I must have a witness by my side at all times to account for my actions."

"You mean murder?" I asked.

"Yes," he answered.

"Go to Harvard, eh?"

"That's where this all happened," he said quickly. "At a cocktail party." He took the *Coronet* magazine from me and leaned back in his seat. "I suppose you want to hear all about it?"

"Well now I . . ."

"My roommate and I considered ourselves the archgivers of cocktail parties, but not, mind you, the usual cocktail party. To us, four walls, a table with a punch bowl on it, glib-talking drinking friends and pretty girls was just the start. A party to be a huge success had to have something more. Do you follow me?"

"Yes, I see," I said, but I wasn't sure. I didn't have much time to think about it because my seat partner continued quickly.

"We decided that what a cocktail party needed was a motif, a raison d'être, a symbol, a stage setting, something to set it on a high plane of entertainment."

"Like a naked girl in a large punch bowl, like at the Rotary Club stag parties?" I asked eagerly.

"Exactly," he stated.

"Well now," I started, leaning back to start in on our famous party last June.

"Our first two parties were huge successes," he interrupted. "The first party had as its motif a pack of my roommate's father's beagles, all twenty-five of them."

"Beagles!" I shouted, dumbfounded. "You mean those fox-hunting hounds?"

"They were marvelous," he said with a half-smile of remembrance on his lips. "Superb. The guests talked about the party for weeks. The only one who complained bitterly was our biddie the next morning, but then she's always complaining."

"But what the hell sort of party is that?" I asked.

"Our next party," he said, ignoring me, "was not quite as successful. It had as its motif tens of suggestively shaped gourds, squashes, and balloons hung about the room. Their effect, unfortunately, was lost due to a thick fog of smoke from an Egyptian incense pan that got out of hand."

"Brother, you must be nuts," I suggested.

"All the trouble started," he continued, "with our third cocktail party, which we had last week. We decided to give one that had a musical instrument as a motif."

"Ah, an accordion player," I suggested.

"So we decided upon a tuba player," he continued without a break. "We called up an orchestra agency and asked for the oldest tuba player they had, along with the biggest tuba on hand. They agreed and at five o'clock the next day their man showed up at our room. The agency had done a good job. The tuba player was a thin little man in his late sixties with a clubfoot, threadbare clothes, horn-rimmed glasses, and the biggest goddamn tuba you ever saw. He was perfect. My roommate and I hugged each other in delight, dressed him up in a hunter's costume, stuck a top hat on him and put him out on display with instructions to play when the guests arrived."

My seat partner started to laugh. "Have you ever heard 'Pack Up Your Troubles in Your Old Kit Bag' played on a tuba?"

"I've heard it played on a piano," I answered.

"Well, that was all this poor fellow could play. He played it for three straight hours, that low ompa-pa-pa-pa coming in over the tinkle of cocktail glasses and chatter like a funeral dirge. It was the most priceless, beautiful thing I've ever heard."

He started to laugh again, then his face grew serious. "It was after the party we got an inkling of what was to come. The last guests had left, still talking about our cocktail coup; left were only half-empty glasses with cigarettes floating in them, and our tuba player. He looked pretty bedraggled. His coat was mussed, his top hat—with a placard someone had stuck in it with the words *Grand Marshal* on it—was tilted over one ear, and he looked pretty worn out. We went up to him, and while my roommate was paying him off, he *thanked* us, thanked us for what he said were the finest three hours of his life.

"Neither my roommate or I," he continued, "could understand it. He had been laughed at, had had martinis poured down his instrument, had to empty the tuba of old socks, cigarette butts, one golf ball, an umbrella, and two volumes of Proust. And yet all he could do was thank us and apologize for only knowing one tune. He kept saying, 'You have re-established my faith in the tuba—never before have I heard it used as a solo instrument. Oh, if I had only brought my music along and played all night.' He got almost hysterical, and it was all my roommate and I could do to get him to leave.

"We all thought that was the end of it, but it wasn't. He called us up the next day and wanted to know when we were having another party. We said not for a long time, which infuriated him. He told us we had been placed in the role of Henri Satie with 'Les Six' and it was our beholden duty to present this great new solo instrument to society. He called us day after day; he'd pop out at us from behind corners, in the dining rooms, even in classes, and play 'Pack Up Your Troubles in Your Old Kit Bag.' He even learned another tune, 'Pop Goes the Weasel,' and he organized a band of what he called downtrodden instruments to play it. He became a frightening millstone around our necks.

"The great climax came last night. My roommate and I had just retired for the night when we heard a frightful cacophony outside the window. We looked out to see our tuba player surrounded by two contrabassoon players, a French horn, and an Egyptian ceremonial drum. We stood it through their rendition of 'Pack Up Your Troubles in Your Old Kit Bag,' but when they started in on 'Pop Goes the Weasel,' my roommate went berserk. He picked up a sofa that weighed two hundred pounds and heaved it through the window. There was one last shrieking belch of sound and all was quiet.

"When we looked out the window the next morning, we saw the

sofa and beside it a beaten-up tuba. It wasn't enough for my roommate. He yelled out that by God that bastid would buy another tuba, and he got so stricken with the idea that he picked up a silver corkscrew and ran into the streets.

"So there you have it," my seat partner said. "That's why I've given you my name and address and asked you to remember the time. I don't trust my roommate under his present state of mind."

"Sounds pretty preposterous to me," I said, which was exactly what I thought.

The Saxophone Player

by George A. Plimpton (1948)

Donald looked at the address again and reluctantly rang the
doorbell.

"How the hell am I going to ask him?" he wondered. He shuffled
his feet and stared at the number on the door. "Maybe he's not in,"
he thought eagerly, half-turning, but he remembered the importance of his mission and stood waiting.

The door opened a half inch and an eye peered out at him. "Yes?"
came a voice muffled by the door.

"Hello," said Donald cheerfully. "May I come in?"

"Who sent you?"

"A man by the name of Cappy Williams—said he knew you in
the old days."

The eye looked at him carefully. "Anybody with you?"

"No, sir."

The door opened wide enough for Donald to squeeze through.
Nobody saw him enter. The door snapped shut quickly behind him,
catching a corner of Donald's seersucker jacket.

"Hey, my jacket's caught in the door."

"Well, pull it loose. You're not catching me opening up that door
again."

Donald tugged at his jacket. It was jammed in tight.

"Bother," said Donald. He pulled again. There was a slight rip-
ping sound. "Think I'll just take it off and let it hang there," said
Donald with a weak smile. He skinned out of his jacket. "Get it
when I leave." The jacket flopped against the door, two pens and a
fifty-cent piece falling out of the pockets and clattering on the floor.

"Jesus, cut the racket. Want to wake up every bull in the neighborhood?"

"Oh, no," said Donald. "Are you Irvin Montague?"

"Yeah."

"Well, here I am," said Donald cheerfully, looking around.

The living room in which he was standing looked like any other except there was a corpse over in a corner with a sheet half over it. Beside it was sitting a man with a fedora pulled down over his eyes, snoring slightly, a bandaged leg up on a stool. Donald had expected at least a few test tubes—maybe even an X-ray machine.

"You are Irvin Montague—a doctor of sorts?" he asked.

"Certainly."

"Well, this is a matter of some delicacy," continued Donald, looking at the man with the fedora.

"Don't be bothering yourself worrying about that bum," said the doctor. "Talk up, mac. What's your trouble? An abortion, maybe?"

"Oh, no," said Donald.

The doctor looked crestfallen. "Gunshot?" he asked severely.

"Heavens!"

"Corpse disposal?"

"Gosh no."

"Nitroglycerin?"

"Why, what would I want that for?"

"Look, mac," said the doctor. "I ain't got much time. What the hell do you want?"

"Well," said Donald softly, watching the man in the fedora hat. "I'm a student out at the college. Got an exam tomorrow in geography—the geography of South America. Three-hour exam. Got the picture?"

"Yeah," said the doctor.

"Well, the truth of the matter is I've only been to one class this year—a class on the resources of the Upper Amazon basin—sugar, rubber, you know. But about the rest of the course, I just don't know beans."

"What?"

"Beans. So I'm bound to flunk. But if I can get an excuse to miss the exam, I can take it again next fall, see? Study all summer and really smash it for maybe a C.

"Well, I was talking to Cappy Williams the other day, and he told me that long ago you used to mix up some sort of drink for students in my predicament that would make 'em pretty sick right in the middle of the exam. Drink it, you see, and then be carried out. Fine medical excuse. No trouble with the dean's office. Perfect."

"And you want me to mix you up a mickey?" The doctor started to laugh. "After all these years—Holy Christ," he sputtered. The man in the fedora stirred slightly and his eyes opened. "Cut the honking, Montague. You want to wake up every bull in the neighborhood?"

The doctor's laugh stopped as though he'd been choked. "Sorry, nipper boy. Take it easy."

"What do you say, doctor?" asked Donald. "It means everything in the world to me. Just can't go on probation again. I don't know what my family would say."

The doctor took a step toward him. "Clear outa here, punk. Blow."

"Hold on, Montague," interrupted the man in the fedora. "Out on probation, eh, kid?" Donald was asked. "Who are you gunnin' with?"

"Leave him be, nipper," said the doctor. "Just a young college punk."

"I like his style," said the man in the fedora. "Fix him up, Montague, with what he wants."

"Brother, anything to get him the hell outa here." The doctor walked quickly across the room through a door to what Donald decided must be the examining rooms.

"I certainly do appreciate it, doctor," Donald called after him. "Perfectly willing to pay you." Donald sat down in a chair. The world looked pretty bright, he thought.

"The doctor's a neat guy, isn't he?" he asked the man in the fedora.

"That punk? Give him half a chance and he'd turn state's evidence. Damn stoolie."

"My, that's too bad," said Donald. He started to hum a tune he'd been picking up on the saxophone. "La-te-dum-te-dum-te-dum."

"Cut the honking, punk. Wanta wake up every bull in the neighborhood?"

Donald laughed and shook his head. "My dear man, we're in the middle of the city. No bulls. La-te-dum-te-dum-te-dum."

"Cut it!" the man in the fedora bellowed. "Wanta get blasted in the guts with a .45?"

"Uncouth beast," thought Donald as he hummed a quick ending flourish to his tune.

"What a fresh punk." The man in the fedora shook his head. "They're sure turning 'em out pretty fresh these days. What's the doc doin' in there for ya?"

"He's mixing me up a drink. You see, I'm taking this geography . . ."

"Soup, eh? Going to blow a safe. Pretty good for a kid your age."

Donald took an orange Life Saver out of his trouser pocket and popped it into his mouth. "You watch the football team play this year?" he asked.

"I'm not in the bookie's racket," said the man in the fedora. "Gotta spend all my time planning capers. If you don't plan your caper you get it in the gizzard like this poor sap here," and he pointed at the corpse in the sheet.

Donald peered across the room. "I suppose that's one of the doctor's cadavers," he said. "Sure would like to take one home with me and stick it in Peter's bed. Peter's my roommate. What a card." He started to laugh. "Oh my."

"Cut it, punk."

Donald stopped. "Bulls?"

"Yeh—bulls."

What a lovely day for an exam, thought Donald. He wrapped his fingers lovingly around the doctor's little bottle as he walked into the examination room. The worried eyes and the tremulous voices delighted him. Punks, he thought. Bulls. He now rather liked the word. "Bulls," he said half aloud.

He looked each proctor in the eye. Ten minutes from now, one of them would be assisting him from the room. He hoped it wouldn't be the big proctor with the glass eye. But then he could hardly be choosy.

He took a seat in the back of the room. Taking the bottle from his pocket, he uncorked it and drank it quickly. "Peppermint," he whispered.

He had a moment of panic when he couldn't find his pencil. But it turned up in the lining of his coat, and in a big scrawl he wrote his name across the blue book.

Perfect, he thought. *Ten minutes to go—no aftereffects—go out tonight with young Edith and blow my saxophone at the moon.*

The examination arrived. Donald picked it up daintily between thumb and forefinger and read, "Discuss for three hours the resources of the Upper Amazon basin."

"Oh, bother," said Donald. "Oh, dash it." He picked up his pencil, but it dropped from his trembling fingers and rolled on the floor.

A Cover from 1949

Cover by Raymond A. Fitzgerald

La Mouche

by Fred H. Gwynne (1949)

A Call for Subscribers

(1950)

LOUIS JOUVET
RALPH RICHARDSON
ZAZU PITTS
ADOLPHE MENJOU
and their stand-ins;

Messers

SELZNICK
DE MILLE
HITCHCOCK
METRO
GOLDWYN
&
MAYER
and their yes-men;

Mmes

HOPPER
GRAHAM
&
PARSONS
and their ghost-writers;

Read

THE LAMPOON

for its two-line jokes
Give a subscription to your agent!

My Stage Name is ....
....
I get my fan mail at ....
....
....

One year for $2

47

De la Comtesse

by Fred H. Gwynne (1950)

January 31, 1950

Snibbins came into the room and presented me with twenty dollars. He looked apologetic as he explained, "Chesterfields aren't worth very much this season, and he didn't like the idea of the patchwork quilts sewn in over the linings. Not a selling point at all, he claimed."

"My God, doesn't he realize what a patchwork-quilt lining means on a cold wintry night? You shouldn't have settled for less than thirty, but we do need the money." I looked around the room and noticed that all the furniture must have been sold.

Every mail brought ultimatums from haberdashers, the phone company, and the old university itself. Today our Chesterfields had gone; tomorrow it might be the very clothes we were wearing. With the dollar really nothing more than a New Deal disguise for a dime, Snibbins and I had recently come face to face with reality—it was impossible to go through Harvard on $940.72 a year, even if the catalogue did say so.

Snibbins looked particularly sad, tears rolling down his cheeks, staining his regimental tie, dripping down over his tattersall, finally settling in his watch pocket, where they raised havoc with his waterproof, shockproof watch. His gray flannels looked conspicuously mussed—these were the dark pair, which I have always called his "Gray Flannels Number One."

"Dammit," Snibbins said. "It's a question of selling apples on the street or pewter beer mugs from door to door."

"There is a more subtle approach," I commented. "Go from door to door, explaining that you're running some sort of questionnaire, and then suddenly pull out an order blank and a list of magazines—with the extra-bonus-point magazines starred with red pencil—and you tell the person that you are working your way through college and that you must get fifty thousand points by July 30, 1953, in order to qualify for a prize of fifteen dollars, a Mickey Mouse wristwatch, and an all-expenses-paid weekend in Binghamton."

Snibbins answered, "Yes, but I have no sales personality—in fact, I have no personality at all. Besides, there must be an easier way."

I nodded. "What about some sort of work that we could carry on in the room? Perhaps a veterinary and kennel business."

"Against the rules. I've got a daring idea. We'll start a smuggling business on illegal French novels, Henry Miller, Frank Harris, and that sort."

"But what we want is quick money and big money. Thousands, millions of dollars. We don't want a job, Snibbins, what we want is an old-fashioned, American-style, rootin' tootin' payoff."

"Right."

"It's a damn shame those pyramid clubs aren't still going."

Snibbins remembered the bottle of Pernod that he had salvaged from our liquor cabinet, which had gone out last week, and after a few highball glasses of the stuff, we thought ourselves to be not so down-hearted after all—we suddenly discovered all sorts of grand ideas.

And the idea that we finally hit on, well, it was a scheme which makes the A&P look like a fruit stand. The strange thing about it was that it looked just as attractive the following morning. A week later, in the conservative Parisian newspaper of the haut monde, *Le Figaro*, an advertisement appeared in the personals section: "Refined, cultured, young, spirited American gentleman desires correspondence with French lady of considerable means. Object is matrimony, with an American marriage certificate. Do not reply unless you want American citizenship with all its benefits and are willing to pay for it."

A few days later we received a letter that was postmarked from Paris. I remembered Snibbins's venture, and so I ran directly to him—by this time we had even sold what was left of the Pernod—and told him of our success. "Wealth and power at our doorstep," I yelled to him. "We should be able to buy back the Bentley next week." He ripped the letter open, read its contents, and began jumping up and down—at times Snibbins was a rather unstable fellow. He spoke, "Why, it's from French royalty, the Countess de Pigalle, and she sounds really game. She offers us a big kiss behind the ears and three million francs to boot!" This was good news, I said to myself. "Why, that's ten thousand dollars—we're solvent once again! Listen to this! She says it will be fine if we simply meet her in New York, sign the necessary papers, and then send her off to Reno for the automatic divorce."

"Fine," I said. "Now there's a young lady who knows when she's well off. Get her over here immediately."

The sky was blue and the sea was calm when the *Ile de France* sailed up the East River and into her berth. It is always a fair day and a calm sea when any modern steamship enters port, not to be confused with the rough, stormy seas which one finds when reading about the grand old days of clipper ships and fine old British gentlemen traveling to Australia to replenish their fortunes and pay their respects to Lord Poppitsford, the governor-general.

After a few toots of the ship's whistle and one prolonged blast of the ship's horn, which discharged a threatening tremolo, the gangplank was lowered, the captain stared down from the bridge, the crowds cheered as they saw their friends, and the ship's parrot commented "*Les Américains, quels foux!*"

The Countess ran swiftly down the gangplank, embraced us tenderly as only a French countess can do, shoved the three million francs into Snibbins's hand, whispered, "*Je t'aime, je t'aime,*" and finally asked, "Are you the young men who are to meet the Countess de Pigalle?"

We rushed the Countess to a small uptown café called Au Cheval Pie, which always reeked with French atmosphere, with a Edith Piaf–ish chanteuse repeating the Marseillaise over and over again, with waitresses who would always whisper, "Allo, bébé," in your ears, and the tip, of course, conveniently figured into your bill.

This remembrance of gay Paris should be enjoyable to our Countess, so we thought, and she made herself very comfortable in a cane-backed chair. After unloading a cigarette vending machine into her purse, she ordered an ale and a dish of pretzels. Our Countess had turned out to be a different sort of person than what we expected.

That evening we went to every place with a French name in town: Au Cordon Bleu, Café de Paris, Café de la Paix, Chez Pierre, Chez Mao Tse-Tsung. Going to the hotel in the early morning, the Countess, who was sitting up straight in the Skyview Taxi, suddenly turned to us and commented, "I sure as hell wished you guys had taken me to some American joints tonight. What about going to them in Reno, Snibbie?" she asked.

By this time, she had persuaded Snibbins to go to Reno with her. He did not need much persuasion, for he wanted to end any marriage with our Countess as soon as possible and with all certainty. In the afternoon, I said good-bye to them at LaGuardia Field, and Snibbins also gave me my half, five thousand dollars.

I hastened back to school, got the Bentley out of hock, bought a case of Pernod for Snibbins's return, and refurnished the rooms in standard Victorian. When I opened the mailbox, dozens of letters from France slipped out. I put them in a little pile on Snibbins's desk and considered affaire d'amour a fait accompli. By this time, the days were going by very quickly, days turned into months, months into years, years back into months. The Pernod looked rather good, and, as any roommate of Snibbins would have done, I decided to try the new batch out. "Good old Snibbins," I kept saying to myself, bottle after bottle. I fell asleep, and dreamed that I was a French count in the court of Louis XIV, who resembled Snibbins quite a bit. I had a strange sensation of being beheaded, which is not a comforting feeling at all. I felt confused and was awakened by a noise at the door.

I opened it, and noticed a telegram and the morning paper. All it said was, HOPE YOU ARE STILL A FRIEND AND WILL PLAY ALONG. What could this mean? I asked myself innocently. Perhaps old Snibbins is playing some game. Then I noticed the newspaper. The headlines explained the telegram. HARVARD STUDENT DIVORCES COUNTESS, they screamed. NAMES ROOMMATE AS CO-RESPONDENT.

Moon Comix

by Fred H. Gwynne (1951)

Hold Up

by John H. Updike (1954)

Although French Calder's Service Station and Ford Agency was a place everybody in town stopped by from time to time during the day, French himself was often lonely, especially in the dead hour between nine thirty, when all those going to work had got there, and eleven o'clock, when the earliest lunch hours commenced. Even after nine years of tending station by himself, French still liked company. Some garage men feel at home with cars, but French said he'd rather talk to people any time. People said French should have been a doctor.

So he was glad to see the Nixon boy cross Route 328 and head for the gas station. Young Nixon was walking along the drainage ditch, scuffling his feet and dressed up in good clothes. "Hello, Jim," French said. "How come you aren't at work?"

"Quit," Jim said, studying his knuckles and picking at one of them with a fingernail.

"Quit, you say?" French tried to keep his voice down, so the curiosity wouldn't show. "And here I thought you were having a good time, learning a man's trade. If I had learned a man's trade now, I wouldn't be stuck here. My dad, he always thought things would take care of themselves. 'All things come to him who waits,' he used to say. So he just let me have my head when I was a youngster." French paused and smiled. "What'd you quit for?"

When Jim Nixon frowned, his eyebrows seemed to get heavier and hang more over his eyes.

Jim thought slow. He was heavy in everything he did and always afraid of making a mistake. He never said much for fear of embarrassing himself. "I just quit."

French ducked down and picked up an oily rag and rubbed

53

around his hands with it. "Don't think I can't understand," he said. "A young man right out of high school doesn't care to work himself to death right off. Even a powerful boy like you gets tired. No need to apologize, Jim. I would've left this job many a time if my father wasn't dead and it was either sink or swim with me. 'Sink or swim,' my dad said before he died . . ."

"I liked the work fine. I'm not afraid of any work." Jim spoke a little louder than before.

"Must admit I thought you were getting along. Ben Youngers said he thought you were coming along. 'The boy takes his time,' he said to me just the other day, 'but what he does, he does his best to do right.' He never thought you'd quit on him. But then, I know Ben Youngers, and I know he works his new men hard and wants them to measure up. That's the way it is in any trade, Jim. They want you to measure up at first. Can't say truthfully I care for Ben myself personally, but . . ."

Jim took a step forward and for a second stared French in the eye. "I like Ben fine. I didn't quit because of Ben or, or anybody."

"Then what did you quit for?"

"Look, French, I can't stand here talking all day. Let's go inside."

"Sun getting you?" French asked politely. "Now, me, I work inside all day, sometimes until ten, eleven at night, and I'm always grateful for a chance to get outside in the air. But then, as you get older, the sun bothers you less. When I was your age, I wouldn't've liked it either, all day in the hot sun, lugging boards and taking lip off Ben Youngers."

"I like the work fine, and Mr. Youngers too." Jim touched his coat pocket and glanced toward the road. "I want a candy bar."

"A candy bar! So that's what you're after. First time I ever knew you to have a sweet tooth. Doesn't do your teeth good, you know." As French walked into the cool of the garage, he noticed how close Jim kept behind him. The candy was kept in a glass case in the corner, beyond the grease pit and beside the rack for the tools.

"What kind do you want?"

"Any kind."

"Anything? Wish all my customers were as unparticular as you. I could give you some Nibs, except they pull the fillings out of teeth. How about a Milky Way? They're soft. Half is, anyway."

"Anything. An O Henry."

When French handed the O Henry to Jim, he saw Jim had a gun in his hand, an old-fashioned pistol, the kind that shot out of a cylinder, still wet with new oil.

Jim blushed and looked away. "This is a holdup," he said.

"Don't tell me! A real holdup? I've read about plenty in the papers, but this is the first time I was ever in on one. Want me to stick up my hands?"

"Put your hands up."

French stretched his hands toward the ceiling and wiggled the fingers a little. "How's this?"

"Don't reach for anything like that air hose overhead."

"Jim, that's shrewd of you. I wouldn't have thought of that myself."

"Cut it out. Just give me the money."

"Why, you know I will. And there must be over three dollars change in the candy case. I'll give it to you all, not to mention the nickel that candy bar's worth."

Jim threw the candy bar on the cement floor.

"I aways knew," French said, "you weren't the sort of boy to ruin his teeth on a lot of candy bars. Why, I bet that was just a what-eyecallit, a subterfuge—that's it. A subterfuge to get me inside."

Jim Nixon waved the gun toward the tool chest. "Isn't there some bills in one of them drawers?"

French beamed. "Jim, you really surprise me, you really do. Who said you were dumb? Lot of young men wouldn't've taken notice where I keep the bills. Some of them could be in here a thousand times and wouldn't know where the big cash was kept."

Jim shifted the gun into his other hand and looked at it as if it was a puzzle he had to solve. Then he pointed it at French's stomach and with some resolution said, "Get it for me, French. I don't want to hurt you. Just get the money for me."

"Jim, I'd like to. But my hands are still up in the air."

A bell over Jim's head rang. He wheeled around, letting the gun hand go limp but making a fist out of the other.

French said soothingly, "Just the bell that lets me know when a customer pulls up."

"Don't go," Jim warned.

French smiled and stretched his hands still higher above his head. "Now that's not using your head, Jim. Now you know that whoever's out there's going to come in here if I don't go out. The thing to do is, send me out there to wait on him, but keep me covered with the gun, so if I do anything fishy, like trying to jump in the car, you can let me have it. Now isn't that the sensible thing?" Without waiting for his captor to assent, French lifted the big drop door and walked into the sunlight, blinking slightly. The customer was Fred Snead. Fred married a wealthy widow from Maryland, so he didn't have to go to work like most men. He didn't have to do anything he didn't want to except listen to her. That's why Fred could be around in the middle of the morning. He was probably on his way to Marty Kleinmetz's Grille and Lounge downtown to watch television and drink beer.

"Ten of the regular," Fred called. "Check the oil for me too, would you, French? This damn lemon just drinks oil all day."

"Buicks do that," French said. When he lifted the hood to check the oil, Fred pushed open his door and squeezed out. Fred had gotten fat since he married the widow, not that he was any bean pole when he was single.

"And how's Molly?" French asked.

"Like she always is," Fred answered.

French laughed, because the widow was usually in a bad temper.

Sure enough, the Buick did need a quart, and while French was dribbling it through the funnel, Fred leaned over the fender, wanting to make conversation. To oblige him, French said, "I hear the Nixon boy quit his job with Ben Youngers."

Fred picked a cigarette out of the pack in his shirt—it was one of those gauzy shirts so transparent you could read "Chesterfield" through the pocket—and said, "I bet it's his mother's doing."

"How do you mean?"

"You know how she is. She told Molly Jim was picking up bad habits with Youngers and his men. Guess he sassed the old lady back once or twice. Guess he's starting to think a little for himself."

"You may be right there, about Jim wanting to get out on his own. He's sitting in the station right now, trying to rob me with a gun."

Fred laughed at the joke and asked how much he owed French. It came to $2.90, but Fred gave him three dollar bills and said, "Let's call it square." Some of these men, they get a little money and get the idea they're really high on the hog. When French tried to force a dime on him, Fred Snead wiggled his fat white hand magnanimously and pulled out.

"*What* took so long?" Jim asked shrilly when French returned to the inside of the station.

"I had to act natural, Jim," French explained. "You don't want Fred Snead smelling a rat and calling down a whole fleet of state cops, now do you, Jim?" He snapped his fingers, as if he had forgotten something, then put his hands high over his head again.

"Come on," Jim said. "Give me the money and let me get out of here." He paused and thought, finally adding, "I'll try to send it all back to you when I get the chance."

"Why do you want to leave town, Jim? You belong here. People like you. I like you. The Nixons been living in this town ever since I can remember."

"I hate this town."

"You mustn't hate this town, Jim, even if your mother . . ."

"It's nothing to do with my mother. Forget my mother. I just want to get on a train and forget everybody in this town." He lowered his voice, pleading. "But I promise I'll get this money back to you."

"Now, there's no need to do that, Jim. You've held me up fair and square, and you don't owe me a thing."

Jim sucked his lower lip behind his upper and pushed it out in a pout. "Give me the money. Now. Please."

"Jim, I'm at your mercy, and I'd like to get the key to the drawer with your money in it, but . . ."

"But what?"

"I can't get it with my hands up in the air."

"Oh, lower them, why don't you? Just get the key." He added, "Or I'll shoot."

French said, "Funny. The key doesn't seem to be in the pocket."

Jim lurched at him. "Don't—"

"Try any funny stuff? Now, Jim, you know me better than that. I wouldn't take any chances with a dangerous armed bandit. I just must have left the key in yesterday's overalls, that's all the trouble is. And they're right in the closet over here, waiting to be washed." As he walked to the closet and fished around for the overalls, he said, "Now that you're leaving town, Jim, and I'm financing the trip, you might say, you might tell me what all this is about? Why you quit Ben Youngers and all."

The boy thought a long while before admitting, "My mother made me quit. Said I was picking up bad ways."

French held up the key for him to see. "Looks like it was in the pants I had on after all." As he pretended to unlock the drawer, he said, "She has your best interests at heart, Jim. No matter what kind of women they are, our mothers love us. You have to admit that."

"I guess."

"Yes, indeed, I remember my mom telling my father, 'It isn't right to let the boy run wild. He ought to be learning a trade.' She had my best interests . . ."

"What's that you're doing?"

French raised his eyebrows at the boy's alarm. He had been carefully counting out the money into neat piles, now and then pausing to rub the wrinkles out of the older bills. "Don't shout, Jim. I have your interests at heart. All I'm doing is sorting out the big bills from the little ones. You know these twenties and this fifty are big bills, with special numbers. They might be marked. They're easy to trace. You must have thought of that. So rather than try to trip you up, I'm giving you the small stuff and you can spend anywhere you like in a pile, and keeping it separate from the big stuff you better keep and spend one at a time, each time in a different place, so the FBI can never track you down.

"While we're at it, another important thing. In some towns, wear old clothes and grow a beard if you can. I don't know why you can't. You're over twenty, and it doesn't have to be a real thick beard. In fact, it's better if it's scraggly and common-looking. The next town you hit, shave it off and dress as snappy as you can. That way, they'll never catch up with you, because you'll seem to be a lot of different people. And can you fake a limp?"

"No." Jim made a grab for the money, but French raised his voice so sharply it made Jim stop in surprise.

"You can't! Why, Jim, I don't believe you've put a speck of thought in on this, now have you? I don't know what to think. Well, I can't do everything for you, but sorting these bills this way should help." French touched his fingers to his forehead, shook his head, and looked Jim square in the face. "Jim," he said, "I'm sick of lying to you. I don't have your interests at heart. The real reason that I'm playing with this money is that I'm stalling for time. I've been stalling ever since Fred Snead left. I knew you were watching all the time, so I knew I couldn't get any spoken message through to him. But when I made out his receipt, I wrote across it, 'Help. Police. Robbery,' so the state police should be here any minute. I'm sorry, Jim." French folded his hands before him and bowed his head.

"You must be lying," Jim cried. "I didn't see you write no receipt."

"I'm sorry, Jim. Now that I see how bad you feel, I wish I hadn't. But it's the fact. Remember how the hood was up, so you couldn't see me from inside the station? That's when I did it. You should have seen Fred Snead's face drop!"

Jim dropped the gun into his pocket and started toward the door.

"Where are you going now?" French asked.

"Out. Away, I guess."

"Now, Jim, use your head. What you need isn't a walk. What you need is an alibi. Go on home and tell your mother the whole story, and you and she can swear you've been at home all along. It'll be your word against mine. Now get going."

The boy moped out the door and turned toward home. He didn't even say thanks, he was that tired.

Even before Jim had walked out of sight, the white and silver Ford of the state police pulled up. Nicholson, the beefy corporal, asked for a full tank of gas and added, "Say, Fred Snead's spreading the story downtown that the young Nixon held you up."

French said, "You know Fred's stories."

"Yeah," Nicholson said. He drummed with his fingers on the side of the door, then suddenly grinned and said, "Christ, I'd hate to be in his shoes if his mother ever finds out."

The Different One

by John H. Updike (1954)

CONTRARY to popular notion, writers, not mother rabbits, name bunnies. The mother of the courageous rabbit thought of him only as the different one, the one who gave her the trouble. We shall call him Elwood.

His difference first showed itself one March morning when he and his brothers and sisters were delicate puffs of pink and white. They straggled behind their mother across a stubby brown field to a clump of woods oddly separated from the forest. A chipmunk rustled on a low-hanging branch, and they all skittered.

All, that is, except Elwood. He held his ground, head up, eyes bright, whiskers taut. After a safe interlude, the other rabbits crawled from the underbrush.

"What's the matter?" Elwood said. "What are you afraid of? Nothing happened. Nothing would have happened."

"You don't know for sure, darling," his mother said. "Something might have happened. After this you better hide with us."

"Bosh," Elwood snorted. "You're a bunch of neurotics."

All through the spring and summer Elwood failed to scamper. And since the danger was always a gust of wind, a groaning tree, or a faraway bird cry, he suffered no injury. "Cowards!" he would snarl at his brothers. "Yellow-bellies! Jellyfish!" One day he said, "I can't stand you sniveling weaklings anymore. Good-bye, Mother. I'm going out into the world, where rabbits are rabbits."

But he found rabbits were all the same. "Mice!" he would shout. "Look at me. I never ran from anything. But I'm here, I'm here!"

Once the Hike-for-Health Club came to the forest, and, although the others hid in the undergrowth many yards from the path, Elwood didn't budge. "Hey, look!" called a fat man. "Look! A rabbit!"

61

"Gee! A real one! Bet he's stuffed!" He was fondled, cuddled, cooed at, and given bits of lettuce and carrot.

"Let us put down our furry friend," counseled a wiser head. "Most likely he is scared stiff. Set him free to scamper back to his friends and to enjoy the simple pleasures of the wood."

The rabbits who witnessed this wondered. "Nuts," replied Elwood, pleasantly full of lettuce. "There is no danger. It is all imaginary. The whole world loves a rabbit. You are stupid dolts, running from nothing but yourselves."

Fall, with its dry rust leaves and bare branches and lack of hiding places, came, and the elder rabbits remembered the guns and the dogs and the men in red hats who came in the season. "Horsefeathers. A myth preserved in the liquid hearts of cowards," Elwood scoffed. "They mean no harm. And if they do? Are we not numerous? Can we not run with the doe and jump with the frog? We could easily overpower them."

He took to the stump. "The only danger exists in the dark labyrinths of your tangled minds. We must throw off this restricting cocoon of senseless timidity and emerge the great and wonderful animal we are. Together, under one inspired leader, we must march forward to meet the intruder, and we must conquer him. Fearless, we are invincible."

So one crisp morning in early November, Elwood and a band of converts went forth to defeat a hunting party. "Faith, and a strong heart are all we need," Elwood said. But at the first distant bark of a beagle, the other rabbits forgot Elwood's teachings and fled.

The dogs found one rabbit, standing proudly alone in the middle of a clearing.

Elwood timed his swing perfectly. He hit the foremost dog on the nose, and it staggered back, colliding with two other dogs. Elwood leaped over the scramble into the face of the next of his enemy, nimbly jabbing his foot in the eye of the baffled beagle. Elwood dodged under their legs and bit their ears, and so elusive and effective was he that several of the dogs, made irrational in their pain and confusion, fought savagely among themselves, howling and snarling. The rabbit charged at the horses, made nervous by this unprecedented turn of things. One of them reared back and tossed its rider to the ground. With a few skillful kicks, Elwood reduced the party to a futile, angry pile of horse and man and red coat.

But then he did a strange thing. At the very moment of victory, he turned and ran. He ran the full way home.

His mother and family looked up when he appeared in the entrance.

"Mother," he panted softly. "I've come back. I'm frightened." Elwood stumbled into the burrow, and the sunlight streamed in from the forest.

Fish Comix

by James D. Stanley (1959)

A Cover from 1958

Cover by Morgan D. Wheelock

Frozen Gold

by Shirley Burden (1963)

Without ice we could not mix our drinks or chill our champagne. Without ice we could not watch hockey, ice-fishing, or any other exciting winter-type sports. We could not laugh at humorous incidents at the expense of old people with brittle bones. In short, without ice, life would be no fun.

Where does ice come from? you ask. This miracle substance may be found in all manner of places, but do not let that fool you. The natural habitat of ice is Northern Canada. In fact, ice is Canada's greatest resource.

Day and night, busy natives scurry about the ice factories and refineries of the far north in order to increase an already burgeoning stockpile of ice reserves. The ice, caught in a raw state by hunters using a variety of space-age methods, is brought in for processing. It is then sorted into different grades, from miniature ice cubes (for use in piña coladas) to the low-grade frost found on windows during the winter. Scientists agree that ice likes to go south for the winter, but, as this is not its natural habitat, this trend is temporary, if not fleeting.

The ice is shipped from Fort Rupert (world center of the ice trade) to various parts of the globe, usually via iceberg. Many years ago, this symbolized the end of the harvest, and was accompanied by the singing of traditional shanties, dancing in the streets, and bludgeoning the village elders with large whitefish.

It is only recently, however, that this vast industry reached its present scope. The discovery of the refrigerator played a crucial role in developing the ice trade. Found in a back alley in Barrie, Vermont, where it had been abandoned by a disgruntled inventor in his search for a better way to make fondue, it prevented ice spoilage, thus facilitating ice exports to the southern regions of the United States.

With the widespread introduction of the refrigerator, it was only a matter of time before the world caught on to this marvelous delicacy. It was tried fried, breaded, baked, and broiled, but it was not until somebody tried to preserve it in alcohol that any significant advances were made.

The first mixed drink was a landmark that heralded a new age of man. New perspectives on the world emerged, and lying prostrate on barroom floors became the vogue. This was the age of Joyce and Eliot.

The ice cube, in its transparent, ephemeral glory, played such an important role in these developments that it is assured of a place alongside man's greatest achievements.

Igor Cassini's Christmas

by George W. S. Trow, Jr. (1964)

November 30, 1964

In his own way Igor Cassini, like Knute Rockne and Ida Lupino, is an American folk hero. Notoriously warmhearted (he will often let a fabulous $20,000 gown go for hundreds less if he likes you), he approaches Christmas with a charming ingenuousness. "I still approach Christmas like a small boy," he said to us recently. "Of course, as a small boy I was very, very rich." Here is an article you'll want to save for years and years in that absurd memory book of yours.

As Mummy, the Russian princess, used to say, there's absolutely nothing as chic as Christmas. But Mummy is dead—along with those elegant, aristocratic ways, the noble breeding (barely understood now), and all that money, all that incredible money, money, money, of our youth. And, sad to say, it would almost seem as though Christmas chic were dead too. Deader than Stalin, if you'll permit me my little joke.

Thus, the problem is, outside the context of all those amazing court functions of which I was such an indispensable part, how to have a chic Christmas.

Try these novel ideas:

1. Affect (oh, go ahead) *poverty*! While all your pedestrian middle-class friends scream and shout about the Waring blender they're going to get for Christmas, you steal the show in eye-catching *rags*. Couldn't be simpler, and you can put the pennies you have saved toward something glamorous, like a trip to Chicago.

2. Turn off all the heat and then have a "body warmth" party. This means really close contact with friends you might otherwise drift away from and big savings on that ugly fuel bill.

3. Invite a foreign exchange student to spend the holidays with you. Study his funny foreign way of doing things at this festive time of year, but try not to laugh. If you can't get a foreigner, try a Democrat. Insist that Barry Goldwater spend Christmas Day with you. He's simply heavenly company, and—well—he doesn't get asked out much anymore. If he comes, you'd probably better cancel the "body warmth" party and hide the foreign student.

4. Icicle your eyelids. Now this is fun. Simply take an everyday blowtorch and get rid of your scraggly wasted eyelashes. Then, using any good brand of nose drops, stand in a freezing room and dribble the liquid over your pitiful scarred little eyelids. In mere minutes the most divine icicles will form, covering the whole rotten mess.

The Transcript Strike

by Henry N. Beard (1964)

February 1, 1964

The strike of Harvard by three-dollar-a-year deans seeking better wages deepened last week with the announcement by the Faculty of Arts and Sciences that grades for the academic year ending in January would be postponed indefinitely pending settlement of the dispute. In a statement released last Wednesday, Acting Interim Dean Elmer Green admitted: "Even if the strike were settled tomorrow, the transcript stoppage would last into mid-February." Dean Green also suggested that the widespread inconvenience and delay that have resulted thus far from the strike were small in comparison to the confusion that could result if the strike is prolonged beyond the January exam period.

"You ain't seen nothing yet," he predicted.

The work stoppage involves three deans who are paid one dollar a year for their services. Their previous contract with the university expired on midnight, December 31, and they walked out of the annual New Year's Eve party at the Faculty Club at 8:30 a.m., on January 1, to protest low wages and lack of fringe benefits. Although the deans had staged a marked slowdown in their work during the preceding weeks, the college claimed to be completely taken by surprise at the sudden move. Attempts to keep the deans on the job while the dispute was arbitrated failed, and while negotiations proceed behind closed doors at the Hotel Commander, the country's oldest college is without its top deans.

F. Skiddy von Stade, speaking for the deans, revealed at a press conference this week that they were seeking a contract agreement on the basis of a $2.30 package which includes a basic wage rate increase of two cents a week this year to be followed by an increase to three cents a week next year. The deans are also demanding a pension plan, with retirement benefits of eighteen cents a year at age seventy, and provisions for overtime. Dean von Stade called a university package offer of $1.20 "totally unacceptable" to the deans and vowed to continue the stoppage "until Harvard Yard thaws." "We will not be intimidated," he declared. "The college is to blame for this situation, and the college must solve it." Asked to comment on the stage of the negotiations and on Dean Green's role, Mr. von Stade declined in both cases. "Ask Elmer," he suggested.

In a joint communiqué issued from strike headquarters in Harvard Hall, spokesmen for the university announced that Harvard would not increase the settlement offer that the deans rejected. "Massachusetts has always had a low pay scale," the communiqué stated. "Ted Kennedy, for example, served as attorney-general in Suffolk County for a dollar a year, and several legislators have done so as well. The college can no more afford unreasonable labor costs than the Commonwealth." The communiqué also stated that the deans had turned down a university offer to submit the dispute to arbitration and fact-finding. Sources close to the negotiation say that the discussions have apparently broken down over the issue of automation as well. The deans have allegedly demanded, and Harvard has refused, consideration of a proposal to replace their administrative and advisory duties with computers to release the deans from repetitive drudgery, thus freeing them to concentrate on their ceremonial functions.

In an interview shortly after the strike began, Professor Samuelson of MIT outlined the deans' dilemma in a series of statements and graphs representing their financial predicament. "The economic position of these deans vis-à-vis the rest of the economy and vice versa is very unequal, viz, the huge discrepancy between the deans' take-home pay and that of related personnel; for, when we figure their labor market status, their tax situation, their savings-investment curve, and their profit-loss margin, we can clearly see the seriousness of their problem." (See figure 1.) "A dollar doesn't buy what it used to," he concluded.

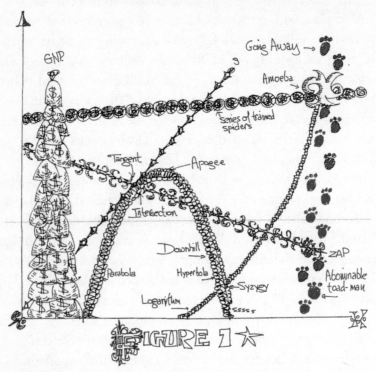

Illustration by David C. K. McClelland

"Living on a dollar a year isn't easy," Mrs. von Stade admitted in another interview at the beginning of the strike. "We get our room and board free from the college, but there are so many other expenses involved these days: the summer house to keep up, the stables to support, all our entertaining, our wardrobes, and miscellanies. We have to budget very strictly to make ends meet: two cents for this, three cents for that, so much for one thing, so much for the other, and so forth. We had a little set aside for a rainy day," she confessed, "but we'll have to live on that now." Asked what would happen if the strike were prolonged, Mrs. von Stade said, "We'll make out somehow; everybody does."

In Washington, Labor Secretary Willard Wirtz called on both sides to reach a noninflationary settlement within the presidential guidelines. He labeled the deans' demands "exorbitant" in terms of the 4.8 percent maximum wage increase set down by the Council of Economic Advisers. "This demand amounts to a 250 percent hike in wage rates alone," he charged, peaking at a Rosicrucians' luncheon where he blasted the deans. "We can't afford an inflationary contract agreement; this settlement will affect the entire industry." Later, Secretary Wirtz denied reports that the president was considering releasing part of the stockpile of dollar-a-year men remaining from government administration jobs in World War II, calling the notion "ridiculous." At week's end, as Harvard finished the first deanless exam period in its history, everyone was guessing. It is clearly Harvard's move, and informed sources say President Pusey is planning something dramatic to emphasize the college's inability to pay the costs of the deans' demands, possibly by cutting his own salary to fifty cents a year, possibly making a similar cut in all salaries. In an off-the-record interview, Mr. Pusey declined comment. "No comment," he reportedly said. Other university officials have been unwilling to discuss the matter at all, possibly for fear of reprisals. One of the greatest mysteries of the entire affair remains the *Crimson*'s failure to mention the strike in its daily publication. This news blackout is doubly inexplicable in the light of its spectacular scoop of Harvard's biggest announcement of the decade last spring.

At the same time, feeling among students and faculty alike runs high in favor of the striking deans. Secretaries and administrators who work in University Hall have refused to cross student picket lines, even though they must cross wire fence lines and risk grass-walking violations to do so. So far, the Harvard University Police have reported no arrests. The student demonstrators, carrying signs protesting the low wages the deans receive and chanting "Dean Green is a scab," have marched peacefully around the building since the strike started. Dean Green and the pro tem administration remain unmoved by the demonstrations. "Let them march around until they turn into butter," Dean Green said.

A Cover from 1966

Cover by Stuart A. Pizer

A Call for Subscribers
in the Form of a Dare

(1966)

Kangaroo Laughter

by Henry N. Beard (1967)

My dreams until quite recently consisted in the main of a rerun of an old series in which I am awarded the Legion of Honor, the Nobel Prizes for Peace and Literature, and a Distinguished Service Cross with seven oak-leaf clusters for drowning the Doublemint twins—who I must confess bear more than a passing resemblance to Lynda and Luci Johnson—in a vat of radioactive Bromo-Seltzer, and on occasional bad nights of a pilot film in which I am tied to a mast while the sirens, who in a mild fog could be mistaken for the Johnson sisters, serenade me with cigarette jingles and implore me to come to that land where the cyclops and the harpies play and live off chocolate bourgeoisie and potatoes parvenus.

Then, several weeks ago, the first kangaroos showed up, a fairly docile bunch appearing with inarguable dream logic in an old silent that dealt with the not inconsiderable part I played in the second Battle of Mons and the subsequent ceremonies at which I am awarded a pre-humus Victoria Cross. Thereafter, they became increasingly in evidence until some time last week the entire cast of a thriller—during the course of which I slay a dragon, whose insatiable appetite for Chevrolets poses a peril of some proportions to our way of life—consisted of kangaroos, including the dragon and the fair damsels it reduces to toasty english at my instigations, parts usually reserved for the daughters of a well-known American public figure. In fact, I recall rather vividly a tendency on my own part toward a vertical perambulation and the inexplicable presence of a rather weighty tail.

Nor were these nasty brutes satisfied with their infiltration of regularly scheduled dreams; they so monopolized most of my prime time with an obnoxious special in which they stood around and laughed in a cackle that beautifully combined the abrasive hysteria of Phyllis Diller and the yogurty chortling of Bennett Cerf. One of the larger ones, who looked like Richard Nixon, just smiled. On particularly bad nights, some wallabies and a dingo or two would get into the act, one of the latter of which, an ugly brute with an Ed McMahon leer, showed up every night after the bars closed to guffaw. It became painfully obvious before too very long that they were laughing at me.

This kangaroo trouble stemmed, I was certain, from a timeless tale, only the punch line of which I could ever remember; it was, significantly, "and the kangaroo said ha-ha." What irresistible raconteur inflicted it on me, I do not recall, any more than I could recall the slightest turn of incident that could possibly have led the beast in question to the fatal boff. My researches among acquaintances whose familiarity with stories of this sort normally guarantees my absence from their salons produced no clue to the erring anecdote, although it did subject me to numerous selections from the lives of other precocious beasts.

I could, of course, have consulted any number of collections of canned comedy, but upon suffering the recitation of an unusually unattractive account of a cat who couldn't or a dog who did, it occurred to me that the possibility of another immortal envoi lodging itself in my memory and bringing other menageries into my slumbers was far from remote. I therefore resolved to reconstruct the history of that marsupial's unfortunate mirth.

The traveling kangaroo and the farmer's dingo showed little promise, and I had a fairly strong suspicion that shaggy-kangaroo stories were something of a dead end as well. I was sure that no bovine Zeus invited some bored Europa to come up and see his kangaroos. "Who was that kangaroo I saw you with last night?" offered little promise, as did all stories involving marsupials marooned on desert islands, puns on their names, and their adventures in bordellos. I also deduced that the "waiter, there's a marsupial in my soup" genre provided insufficient maneuvering room for kangaroos. In this manner I produced a number of third-rate after-dinner jokes with inappropriate punch lines, which I am holding in reserve for a few special friends.

It was at about this point that desperate, dingo-eyed, and tortured by the ominous thumping of massed marsupials drumming in my mind that purely by chance I hit upon the very anecdote which had been the cause of the kangaroo trouble. Last night I received the eighth oak cluster to my D.S.C. for flaying alive two familiar-looking female kangaroos with a wet shaggy dog.

It was, I must confess, a rather disappointing story, and I won't bore you with it.

A Call for Subscribers from the *Lampoon*'s *Newsweek* Parody

(1967)

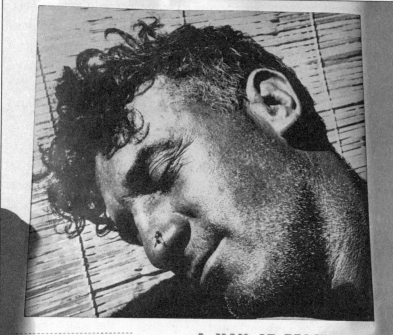

A MAN AT PEACE

Pablos Chees is a Man of Influence. At 16, he made his start selling serapis in New Mexico. Today, at 26, he has expanded his line to include sombreros. To what does he attribute his success? In Pablo's own words, "I read the LAMPOON, and take to heart its witty, incisive commentaries on the current scene."

Would you like to sleep as soundly as Pablo, your mind gently lulled by Lampy? Mind you, it's no coincidence that .02% of America's top business executives read the LAMPOON. Note that! Other magazines claim figures as high as 90%, but we aim at only .02%, the *very top crust*. How can you join this select group? Generally, we require that prospective subscribers submit complete backgrounds on themselves with at least three references, but because this is Leap Year and the backgrounds we receive are usually horribly depressing anyway, we make the following offer. Simply snip, tear or gouge the coupon off this page and send it to us. Or if you want instant attention, send a telegram. (We'll treat it the same in any case, but you'll impress us no end with a 'gram.) Presto! Sit back and wait for 9 of the funniest events you've seen since your wife was caught in the buzz saw.

The price? Gad, man, let's not be vulgar. Be assured it is a pittance compared to what you spend on your secretary. But since you're interested, we refer you to the coupon at left.

Famous Beings School

by John M. Gilpin (1971)

Ever get the feeling you don't know as much as you should about what it's all about? That all-too-familiar queasiness telling you that maybe, just maybe, you're missing out on something pretty big? That you're not, in the words of the poet, "drinking life to the lees" (bottom of the glass) for some reason or other?

Well, stop worrying. In the first place, statistics conclusively prove that you're not alone. In the second place, we here at the FAMOUS BEINGS SCHOOL have a pretty good idea of what you're going through, and—what's more—we can help.

Ever since the human race began, men from all over the face of the globe, from many different walks of life, have been successful in leading happy, meaningful lives. The sailors of ancient Phoenicia, Marco Polo, Frederick the Great, the yeomen of medieval England, many of our American presidents, to name just a few—the list could be extended indefinitely.

And what was their secret? Simply this—they had things to do, and they did them. Well, that doesn't seem like much, you say in a puzzled tone. BUT—it's not that easy for us.

According to current statistics, we live in the most troubled times in earth's history, what with the media, the threat of nuclear catastrophe, pollution, etc.—most of us feel like throwing in the old sponge, taking a rain check on life.

We need something firm, something to hold on to—and statistics tell us that, the Great Riddle of Life being the teaser it is, that "something's" not going to be the same for everybody.

We've discovered that the way to crack the big combination is to learn the lessons of history. And, thanks to the creators of the FAMOUS BEINGS SCHOOL, those lessons are now available in legible, easy-to-understand form. Our series of forty-seven differ-

ent Correspondence Courses, tested and retested to guarantee complete satisfaction, will provide you with a lifestyle you'll be happy to
stick with for the rest of your natural life (and our Statistics Department tells us that chances are you'll pile up valuable points to help
you along when you finally do cash in those chips).

All this in the space of eight short weeks—in the comfort of your
own home—and at minimal cost to yourself.

Sound tempting? Send in the coupon below for your free copy
of our catalogue, at no obligation, of course. And don't delay—our
offer won't expire, but you might.

NAME_____

ADDRESS _____

_____

_____

YES! I *travail* and am heavy laden, and want to hit it big. Send me a copy of your
FREE booklet. I understand that I am under NO obligation at any time. I don't
understand anything else.

FAMOUS BEINGS SCHOOL
0 Freedom Square
Cambridge, Mass. 02138

Understanding Harvard

by Jim Downey (1972)

A word to freshmen

Understanding Harvard

*A straightforward, indispensable guide for young men beginning
their four-year stay at the nation's oldest university*

Part One: Extraneous Introductory Material

Some things about Harvard never change: The sight of good fellows getting up a game of touch by the Eliot House field; the reverential awe of a freshman as he doffs his cap when passing old John Harvard; the sounds of a few of the lads gathered round a table for an evening of drink and song at the Fly; the swarms of worried students taking that extra quaff from the old College Pump the night before finals. And as surely as typhus follows a drink from this self-same College Pump, every year freshmen coming to Cambridge for the first time bring with them a host of distorted images and misapprehensions concerning the College. Some of these "Harvard myths," such as the commonly held belief that "soul-kissing" can lead to pregnancy and even death, are easily confuted. But other, more insidious lies continue their hold upon young minds at Harvard, frustrating the work of counselors and resisting our best efforts at contravention.

In the hope that something can be done to dispel the haze of flim-flam which hovers about the minds of Harvard freshmen, haunting them throughout their college years and hampering their breathing and vision, we have here presented some of the most frequently asked questions about the College, and have, we think, dealt with these myths in rather short order. I think we shall see the last of them.[1] Indeed, it would truly be tragic if, through a want of action on the part of those who should know better, this thick, noisome fog of misunderstanding continued to cloud the minds of yet another group of freshmen, leaving them continually bumping into things and cutting themselves while shaving.

You may, after reading this article, wish to pass it on to a friend or to organize discussion groups with your classmates to talk over the questions raised here. I myself think that this is a fine idea, and I say "Good luck to you." You may also develop other uses for it, and indeed you are perfectly free to do so. In any case, it would truly be misfortunate if this useful educational tool were to be denied the attention it deserves.

Part Two: Some Questions
Frequently Asked by Harvard Freshmen

I've heard that the academic pressures at Harvard are really intense, and I'm afraid that I won't be able to keep up with my work. Are these stories true?

Hardly. Even students of modest academic aptitude (say, 750 verbal, 765 math on the S.A.T.) can generally graduate in the top two-thirds of the class with a bit of hard work and a few sacrifices in their social lives. It's tough (no one ever said that it was going to be easy), but far from impossible. I am reminded of the student back in the '50s who got into Harvard with 1450 S.A.T.'s (he was an All-American football player), and who eventually graduated in the top three-fourths of his class. As I've said, it's not easy, but it can be done in the great majority of cases.

---

1 Members of our staff were heard to comment more than once, "So much for the pseudologists and mythologers," while another maintained that "It looks like the Groves of Academe have been cut and weeded once and for all."

What about the work load? I understand that it can really be heavy for freshmen.

Nonsense. Four or five good hours of study a night is plenty for even the mediocre student described above—provided, of course, that he plans his program carefully. Students who err in constructing their plans of study (for example, those who sign up for the wrong course by accident), or those who simply discover themselves to be of less than average ability, will choose to spend a great deal more time on their schoolwork or suffer the consequences.

What consequences?

Social stigma, loss of scholarship funds, inferior dormitory accommodations and seating at football games, and, in certain cases, general social ostracism.

I've been told that a great many freshmen drop out of Harvard each year because of the academic pressures. Is this true?

Not very. In point of fact, only 20–25 percent of the Harvard freshman class drops out of school for academic reasons, and even this rate decreases for a given class over a four-year period. By the time you are a senior, for example, the drop-out rate for your class will have withered to 10 or 12 percent per year. Generally, almost 900 students from an entering class of 1600 can expect to graduate; hardly what one would call a bleak picture.

As a freshman, I'm taking a variety of courses, and I'm beginning to have doubts about sticking to my pre-med program. Is this unusual?

This uncertainty concerning your major *is* a bit unusual, but it will probably disappear within a few weeks, so there's no cause for alarm on your part. And you'll be reassured to know that virtually all (96 percent) Harvard students who graduate stick with the majors they signed up for on their admission applications and N.M.S.Q.T. test forms. So stop worrying and get to work. If, however, these doubts about your program persist, perhaps you would do well to take a few years off from school to think about it, lest you completely and irrevocably waste your college years.

If, after thinking about it for some time, I decide that I'd like to change my major, will this be possible?

Yes, if it's done before the end of your freshman week. After this point there's not much that anyone can do for you, unless you wish to bring the matter to the attention of your Senior Tutor.[2]

Is it true that each year Harvard's freshman class is brighter, more active, and more talented than the last? If so, where will this spiraling rate of competition end?

You may not realize it, but you've just uncovered one of Harvard's most persistent myths. I don't know where or how it started; I can only tell you that it is completely and totally *false.* As a matter of fact, this year's freshman class is one of the *least* distinguished in Harvard's history. Students from the Class of '76 appear rather uninquisitive, intellectually sluggish, and politically conservative as compared with those of earlier years. In addition, the proportion of National Merit Scholars in the class has dropped this year to 88 percent; not bad, but certainly nothing to write home about.

Why is this year's freshman class so mediocre as a group?

It would be too difficult to go into all the reasons at length here; suffice it to say that a decrease in the overall number of Harvard applicants and in the quality of these applicants last year forced the Admissions Committee to lower its standards considerably. Indeed, last year was an easy one for Harvard applicants. Exact figures are

2 Freshmen have no Senior Tutor. (Ed.)

hard to obtain, but friends in the Admissions Office have told me that upwards of 30 percent of this year's freshmen were admitted "simply in order to fill the class." The tragedy of all this, of course, is that these students have almost no hope of graduating from the College; in time they will simply be unable to keep up with the work. Indeed, at the time of this writing many have already dropped out.

Do certain quotas in admissions have an appreciable effect on the overall quality of a freshman class?

You've hit the nail on the head. Yes, the total intellectual caliber of a Harvard class is lowered by such factors as the presence of famous and/or wealthy people's sons in the group, and heavy recruiting of students from the Midwest and South. If you know of any really dull students in your class (if not, you'll probably be hearing about them in the dining hall soon), say in the 1350–1400 range on the S.A.T., it's a safe bet that they fit into one of these categories—unless, of course, they happen to be some of the Admission Committee's "random picks," or as they are more commonly known, "mistakes."

Are there many such students in a given class?

No, thank God. Generally the rate of "mistakes" in the class runs no higher than 5 percent.

How do these "mistakes" make it into the freshman class at Harvard?

There are many reasons: letters of acceptance sent to the wrong address, cases of mistaken identity, misplaced or jumbled test scores. There is a considerable margin for error, especially when admission applications are being read by exhausted graduate students and seniors who in many instances, if you'll pardon my saying so, couldn't care less about who goes to Harvard. (In one case I knew of personally, several students were admitted who had not even applied. As a matter of fact, one of them was dead.)

As a freshman, I'm worried about taking courses with upperclassmen. Is this a reasonable fear?

Definitely. It is impossible to overemphasize the fact that freshmen *should not* take courses designed primarily for sophomores, juniors, and seniors. There are many perfectly good, general courses (Chem 20, Nat Sci 10, and History 132, to name a few) for freshmen to take without getting in over their heads. If you can swing it, your best bet is to take four courses in elementary Spanish. And above all, don't be tricked into taking middle-group expository writing courses as a freshman, and avoid some of the easy-sounding General Education offerings. More freshmen have flunked out of Harvard because of courses such as Nat Sci 5 and Soc Sci 137 than those in power at this university would care to admit (my own guess would be 15 percent of the class). If you are sincerely interested in taking these courses, don't worry; they'll still be around when you're a senior. Of course, if you happen to be in the Honors track of the freshman class, you may disregard this advice, but *proceed with caution.*

What do you mean by the term "Honors track?"

Although you may not be aware of it (you should ask your Senior Tutor for the details)[3], as a freshman you have been placed in an academic "track" to guide your work at Harvard. Briefly, the system works as follows: incoming freshmen are grouped into categories on the basis of their admission application essays, secondary school headmaster's recommendation, and psychological profiles from the S.A.T. test. These data are then collated with the student's real S.A.T. scores and his grade on the summer reading test. Each student is then placed into one of the three academic "tracks": Honors, Grad-School Prep, and General. The explanation of the grading weights assigned to the different tracks is too lengthy to go into here. It is important to remember only that students in different

3 Freshmen have no Senior Tutor. (Ed.)

"Chaplain, even though I failed my first hourly and have been forced to drop out of school, could I still be reinstated for the spring term?"

"No."

tracks receive a different number of "quality points" for the same grades in a given course. Again, consult your Senior Tutor for the details.[4]

What if a freshman feels that he has been placed in the wrong track?

Of course, no one can ever move up a track, but if you feel that your abilities have been overestimated you may drop to a lower one (provided you have the approval of your Senior Tutor).[5] I might also emphasize here that almost all courses are open to all students, whatever their track. However, students in the General group should proceed with caution.

What about freshman seminars?

In general these are to be avoided by freshmen as the work involved is very often too much for a first-year student. Some seminars, however, have proved in the past to be both easy and valuable learning experiences for students. Again, however, students in the General group should proceed with *extreme caution*.

---

4 Freshmen have no Senior Tutor. (Ed.)

5 Since freshmen have no Senior Tutor, they often tend to get the short end of the stick on this and other matters.

I've talked to some upperclassmen who have told me that Harvard has a fairly high suicide rate. What do you know about this?

Stories about Harvard's suicide rates are highly exaggerated, and every year students and their mothers are worried sick on the basis of a lot of loose talk. In point of fact, the suicide rate in the Harvard freshman class rarely rises above the 15–20 percent level, and most of these occur in Thayer and Grays dorms (the rate of attempts, of course, is much higher). So unless you happen to live in Thayer or Grays, stop worrying.

I live in Thayer. What is it about the suicide rate here that I should know?

I wish to emphasize that most stories about Harvard's high suicide rates, with the exception of the two special cases mentioned above, are a lot of twaddle. Don't believe anyone who tells you differently.

What about all the people who seem to be vaguely dissatisfied with Harvard? I'm not talking about potential suicides, but people who just aren't all that happy here.

Now it appears that *you* are exaggerating. A few students may voice some complaints during their first week or so here, but virtually all of them adjust fully to college life by the end of the third week. An insignificant percentage (1–1½ percent) of the freshmen may have more difficulties making this transition in lifestyle, and may even have second thoughts about the Harvard experience itself, but such malcontents and misfits are more to be pitied than despised. There are a few bad apples in every bunch, and Harvard's freshman crop is no exception. These people would probably be better off at some other university anyway.

What should someone do if he begins to have doubts about Harvard?

First of all, the chances are 50 to 1 that he *never will*. Of course, for the type of seriously deranged individual you describe, the University does provide free psychiatric counseling at the University Health Services. However, the extreme danger of the treatments and the social stigma attached to them makes the percentage of students who "cop out" in this manner quite small, generally a little less than one percent.[6]

What other types of services does the University Health Services provide?

One of its more valuable services to the Harvard community is the provision of a psychological folder on each student to all extra-curricular activity leaders, athletic coaches and Club presidents. In addition, once each semester, at UHS "Open House," students are allowed access to any other student's psychological file by presenting their Bursar's cards.

What sort of information do these folders contain?

They are fairly comprehensive records of a student's mental and psychological history, including his S.A.T. scores and reports on his personality and character by his proctor, Senior Tutor, secondary school headmaster, fellow students, teachers, and hometown clergy-man. It's a shame that the only individuals never allowed to see these folders are the students themselves.

You mentioned extracurricular activities above. Is it a good idea for freshmen to participate in an outside activity?

Evidently, for 98 percent of the freshmen at Harvard are active in some extracurricular activity. Indeed, by the end of the fresh-

---

6 "Hopeless cases" needing "special treatment" are generally sent to a branch of the University Health Services Psychiatric Ward known as "Room 13," a place about which the less said, the better.

man year *all* Harvard students are firmly established in their activity, except for those who intend to concentrate on academics during their undergraduate years.

Do many students participate in sports?

Yes, a very high (97 percent) percentage of Harvard students were varsity team captains in high school, so it comes as no surprise that *virtually all* Harvard men continue to participate in intercollegiate athletics throughout their college years. Besides being a necessary and delightful adjunct to studies, sports are an excellent preparation for the yearly general physical examinations required of all students.

What are these general physical examinations?

The criteria change every year, but generally each student must be able to swim 400 yards, do 200 push-ups, lift 1½ times his body weight, and run a mile in under 5 minutes, nothing a student in reasonably good physical condition shouldn't be able to handle.

At times I have difficulties getting along with my roommates. Is there anything I can do about this?

If you find that you are unable to live with your assigned roommates, you should bring the matter to the attention of your Senior Tutor.[7] He can rectify the problem, although you will in all probability be forced to accept inferior dormitory accommodations after moving out of your room. I might also point out here that since students who move out of their rooms are rarely replaced by others, it is in the interests of your roommates to create an incentive for you to move out of the room. This leaves them with an extra single bedroom or what-have-you. So keep this in mind before rashly judging your roommates. After all, there is certainly nothing wrong with wanting a single bedroom.

7 Freshmen have no Senior Tutor. (Ed.)

Are freshmen roommates assigned to each other in a lottery?

Not at all. The university attempts to assign freshmen to roommates with complementary interests and abilities. Thus, in any one room, depending upon the group size, there will be one genius, one moron, one athlete, and one creep; generally it takes roommates only about a week to figure out who is what. But keep in mind that this is the procedure only for setting up freshmen roommate groups. All upperclassmen, of course, are assigned to live together on a lottery basis.

I have already begun to think about what House to apply to this spring, and I have heard a great deal about the special "character" of each House. What can you tell me about this?

The idea of a House "character" is a monumental exaggeration, and every year many students are sadly misled by a lot of loose talk. In general, all the Houses are pretty much alike. It is true, for example, that Adams House members are demonstrably more gifted in music and the fine arts than other students; similarly, Quincy House people are shrewder businessmen than most, and upon graduation earn twice the salary of other Harvard students. Dunster House people are decidedly more with-it politically than the average Harvard student, while those in Winthrop House tend to be snotty, arrogant prep-school types, about whom the less said, the better. Lowell House is almost entirely (90 percent) group-one students, and each year accounts for nearly all Harvard Rhodes Scholarships. Kirkland House, of course, is composed mainly of varsity athletes, and incidentally has the lion's share (45 percent) of the university's homosexuals. Leverett House seems to be a catch-all for Harvard's psychological misfits, while Mather House people are generally the freshmen roommates you'll decide not to live with next year. Eliot House, in most respects, is like any other, although its students show a rate of pleurisy five times the national average, a fact contributing to its recent unpopularity. Finally, Harvard students who live at Radcliffe, in all but a handful of cases, are wimps and twerps. But as I said above, beyond these differences Harvard houses tend to be pretty much the same.

If I find that I don't "fit in" at the House I'm assigned to, may I apply for a transfer?

No.

I've heard that students at Harvard can pretty much do what they want as far as rules governing their social lives are concerned. Is this true?

Yes, thanks to some ground-breaking developments in the recent past, Harvard has indeed loosened up its regulations considerably in this area. This year for the first time daily chapel attendance will no longer be required of all students, and Black freshmen will certainly be glad to hear that the controversial seating plan for minority groups in lecture and dining halls has been almost totally abandoned. In addition, parietals for Harvard students have been relaxed to the point where men may have visitors at almost any time of the day. Females, of course, are never allowed in a Harvard dormitory.

Is there any way of bringing a female visitor into one's room?

In the past, some students have found success in this area by disguising their female guests in a variety of ways, but this has not worked for several years. I'm afraid that the answer to your question is "no."

What about rules governing class attendance?

Generally it is unwise to stay home from class, unless one obtains the necessary papers from the University Health Services or one's hometown clergyman. In larger lecture courses, of course, skipping classes is considerably safer. Your best bet here is to convince a friend to sit in your assigned seat in the lecture hall and to raise his hand when your name is read for attendance. This technique has proved fairly effective for class-cutters in such large courses as Economics 10 or Social Sciences 137 (although freshmen are advised *not* to take these courses). Make sure, however, that your friend stays on the lookout for grad-student monitors, whose function is to prevent precisely this kind of fraud. Whatever you do, *don't make a habit of it.* Sooner or later, they always catch up with you.

You've mentioned before that it is unwise for freshmen to enroll in courses designed primarily for upperclassmen. Is there much contact between freshmen and upperclassmen outside the classroom?

Yes. I'm afraid that you may be sure of that. There are always groups of Uppers out to "haze" the Frosh, so be sure to stay on the lookout for this kind of activity. It is advisable, for example, to learn the words to the school loyalty and to "Fair Harvard" in the event that you are "asked" to give an impromptu "concert" in the Yard for the benefit of the Uppers. In addition, never act smug or self-confident in the presence of upperclassmen, and avoid any activity which might be interpreted as such. Most hazing of Frosh, I hasten to point out, is done strictly in good fun; you may have your books knocked out of your arms more than once, or even receive the "Frosh haircut," but in general you have little to worry about. Since, however, several freshmen have died in the past two years as the result of overzealous hazing, the administration is cracking down on the practice at Harvard. It will be a sad thing when it passes from the College for good.

Is there anything else that freshmen should avoid?

Yes. It is a good idea for freshmen to proceed with extreme caution in their day-to-day economic affairs, for many students at Harvard seem to feel that Frosh were born to be swindled. In fact, one enterprising group of upperclassmen, calling their operation "Harvard Student Agencies,"[8] once made a career of "fleecing the

---

8 If you should run across anyone claiming to represent this organization, report him immediately to your Senior Tutor. In the past, many freshmen have had their rooms robbed by people gaining access to dormitories with H.S.A. "identification" cards.

Frosh." Their operators tried every trick in the book, from manning the registration lines with pickpockets to selling elevator passes to freshmen. A few rather bold students even attempted to "rent" to freshmen the refrigerators which come with all first-year students' rooms. Some freshmen, I am told, actually paid for this "service." But the favorite trick of H.S.A. operators, however, was to convince (often by force or threats of force) gullible freshmen to patronize their "linen agency." Every year some freshmen would pay $40 to have their dirty sheets and towels "cleaned" and exchanged for "fresh" linen (actually someone else's soiled sheets) each week during the school year. It sounds funny until you realize that the "cleaning" end of the operation actually involved refolding and exchanging *dirty linen*. Finally, so many freshmen developed severe skin disorders from sleeping on H.S.A. sheets that the University administration stepped in to stop the operation. I realize that this is an extreme example of the kinds of dangers which face freshmen in their economic affairs, but frauds only slightly less blatant than this have worked remarkably well in the past. Swindlers such as the old H.S.A. operators could well surface once again. A word to the wise.

A Cover from 1973

The Department Store Display

by Ian A. Frazier (1973)

WASP Jokes

by Thomas R. Feran, Jr. (1974)

In clawing their way to their current position in American society, our Anglo-Saxon forebears learned that laughter is indeed
the best medicine. In doing so, they developed a brand of humor all
their own; a light-hearted, sometimes sardonic, sometimes cutting
way of looking at themselves and their foibles. It wasn't long before
other groups joined in the fun and this proud and colorful people
found itself the butt of good-natured gibes at its customs and traits.
In a free country such as ours, where no sacred cow is safe from
having its toes stepped on, the WASPs soon joined in the laughter.
We hope you will, too, no matter what your nationality.

How can you tell when you're in a WASP neighborhood?
The homes are very large and well cared for.

Why do WASPs have such large balls?
Because they find it difficult to hold small intimate gatherings
without slighting family, friends, or business acquaintances.

Two WASPs were out fishing in a rowboat and having phenomenal
luck. "This is such a great place," one remarked, "we should put an
X on the bottom of the boat to mark it." The other WASP chuckled at the obviously facetious remark, and they noted the spot with
cross-hatching on their map.

*What's dumber than a Polack building a house in the middle of the ocean
and an Italian laying the driveway?*
A WASP financing it.

How did the first WASPs come to America?
On the *Mayflower.*

A WASP space official informed his colleague that an expedition to the sun was planned. Amazed, his colleague interjected, "Won't the incredible heat incinerate the spacecraft?" "It's a suicide mission," came the reply.

How many pallbearers are there at a WASP funeral?
Six, although there may be more so-called honorary pallbearers.

Why did the WASP throw his alarm clock out the window?
As a histrionic gesture demonstrating his dissatisfaction with the regimentation of his life.

What do WASPs put on their front lawns?
Sod.

How do you tell the bride at a WASP wedding?
She's the one in the white gown standing next to the groom.

What do you call a garbageman in a WASP neighborhood?
A sanitation engineer.

Did you hear about the new WASP tires? They get over 70,000 miles and give excellent control.

How many WASPs does it take to change a lightbulb?
Two. One to actually change it and one to hold the ladder for him.

A WASP went to pick up a pizza. The counterman at the pizza parlor said, "Do you want it in six or eight pieces?" "Better make it six," the WASP said. "I'm sharing it with five friends."

Write your own WASP jokes! Here are a few "setups."
What is the national bird of England?
How do you get ten WASPs into a Renault?
Who is the most feared man in a WASP neighborhood?

And here are some surprise answers:
Henry—in the Eighth
A stiff upper lip
Queen Kong
Wash Georgington

Notes from the Under-Grateful

by Patricia A. Marx (1974)

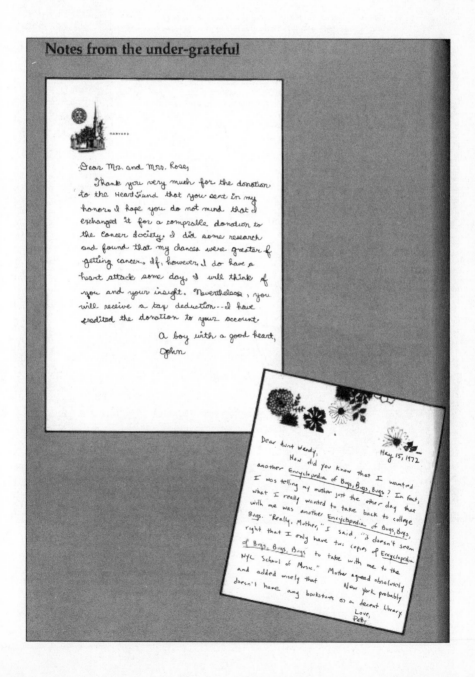

Notes from the under-grateful

Dear Mr. and Mrs. Rose,

Thank you very much for the donation to the Heart Fund that you sent in my honor. I hope you do not mind that I exchanged it for a comprable donation to the Cancer Society. I did some research and found that my chances were greater of getting cancer. If, however, I do have a heart attack some day, I will think of you and your insight. Nevertheless, you will receive a tax deduction--I have credited the donation to your account.

A boy with a good heart,
John

Dear Aunt Wendy,
May 15, 1972
How did you know that I wanted another Encyclopedia of Bugs, Bugs, Bugs? In fact, I was telling my mother just the other day that what I really wanted to take back to college with me was another Encyclopedia of Bugs, Bugs, Bugs. "Really, Mother," I said, "it doesn't seem right that I only have two copies of Encyclopedia of Bugs, Bugs, Bugs to take with me to the NYC School of Music." Mother agreed absolutely and added wisely that New York probably doesn't have any bookstore or a decent library.
Love,
Patty

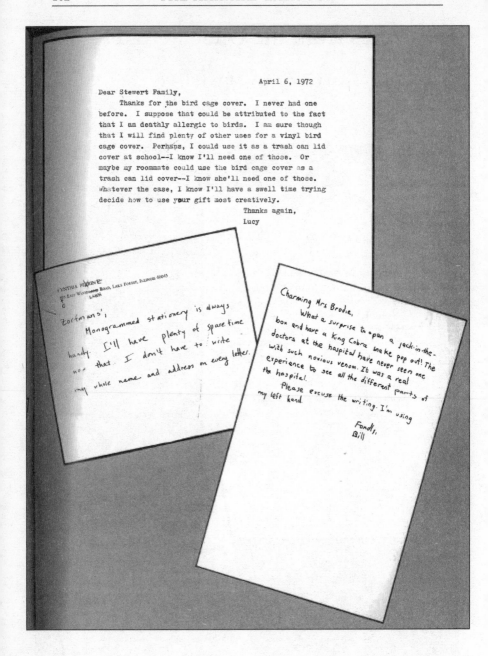

April 6, 1972

Dear Stewert Family,

Thanks for the bird cage cover. I never had one before. I suppose that could be attributed to the fact that I am deathly allergic to birds. I am sure though that I will find plenty of other uses for a vinyl bird cage cover. Perhaps, I could use it as a trash can lid cover at school--I know I'll need one of those. Or maybe my roommate could use the bird cage cover as a trash can lid cover--I know she'll need one of those. Whatever the case, I know I'll have a swell time trying decide how to use your gift most creatively.

Thanks again,
Lucy

CYNTHIA PERRINE
East Woodward Road, Lake Forest, Illinois 60045
LAWN

Zorfmans',
Monogrammed stationery is always handy. I'll have plenty of spare time now that I don't have to write my whole name and address on every letter.

Charming Mrs Brodie,
What a surprise to open a jack-in-the-box and have a King Cobra snake pop out! The doctors at the hospital have never seen one with such noxious venom. It was a real experience to see all the different parts of the hospital.
Please excuse the writing. I'm using my left hand.

Fondly,
Bill

On the Road

by Walter S. Isaacson (1974)

Pleasant City, Ohio—In which a reporter for a major news network discovers America, life, and the world around him.

Walter Cronkite: For the past six years, our reporter Charles Kuralt has been traveling around America reporting on what gives true meaning to the lives of people like you. This report will be his last. For in America's heartland, Charles Kuralt has at last found America's heart.

[*Charles Kuralt is shown standing in front of a wooden-frame bar with a horseshoe-shaped green neon sign in the window. Red letters proclaim* Ladies Invited. *Through the window comes the glow of a TV set over the long wooden bar.*]

Charles Kuralt: Interstate 70 and Interstate 77 intersect at Pleasant City, Ohio. Even if they did not, the Horseshoe Bar and Lounge (Ladies Invited) would still be here. We know that. It was here before the interstates were. And time, like the trucks that rumble by here, flows forward.

[*Camera switches inside. A customer in sixteenth-century garb is sitting at the bar; the waitress addresses him.*]

Barmaid: Hey, Bacon, what you having?
Bacon: Ahh, hell. How would I know? I just got up.
Second Customer: What's up, Bacon?
Bacon: Me. Weren't you listening?
Charles Kuralt: Like the Bacon who didn't write Shakespeare's plays?
Bacon: I did write Shakespeare's plays.

[*At this moment Bacon's body is brushed by the boastful Baptist breasts of the barmaid.*]

Barmaid: Excuse me for being so alliterate.

Bacon: Illiterate?

[*She slaps him.*]

Bacon: Bourbon and Coke.

Barmaid: Kid's stuff.

Bacon: With no ice.

Barmaid: Bush league.

Bacon: Make it a double and skip the Coke?

Barmaid: That's better. Now let's try to avoid excessive dialogue in this celluloid mood painting of life in America.

Charles Kuralt: Earlier this evening an amazing thing happened. On this TV set above the bar flickered a rerun of *Peter Pan*. When the time came for the viewers to clap to save Tinker Bell, nobody moved. They stared blankly. In spite of Mary Martin's begging, they simply watched. And Tinker Bell faded away. Nowadays life is seldom as you would expect it. Ten years ago this would have caused a furor. There would have been angry letters to the editor, jammed TV-station switchboards, marches in New York City, pique in Darien, Connecticut. B. F. Skinner's pigeons would probably have quit playing Ping-Pong. The world would be changed. Tonight, no one cared. On the road we have found this—the American Spirit.

Bacon: Somewhere on the Left Bank of the Seine River, a Parisian artist is watching a hair, dark and thick, growing out of his knuckle.

Barmaid: So what?

Second Customer: So what?

Bacon: It's sort of the Human Condition.

Barmaid: Or a symptom of it?

Second Customer: Or a metaphor for it?

Charles Kuralt: This is Charles Kuralt, at the end of the road, in Pleasant City, Ohio.

Walter Cronkite: And that's the way it is, Friday, December 21, 1973.

"Second Coming" Doesn't Set the World on Fire

by Stephen M. O'Donnell (1975)

The seven seals opened last night and the much-heralded, much-gossiped-about, highly anticipated End of the World began its run. This reviewer was not impressed. It is the clumsiest apocalypse I have ever viewed, and possibly the most under-rehearsed spectacle since the dawn of time. Bogged down by heavy-handed symbolism and millions of actual deaths, the Second Coming of Our Lord Jesus Christ would have done better to stay a few extra months in New Haven.

Rumors of budget troubles plaguing God's version of the disaster epic have clearly been dispelled by the lavish settings and special effects. These alone, however, cannot salvage the event from its tedious theme and melodramatic direction.

The show is hurt by a whole slew of technical mix-ups that are very distracting—rainbows look like emeralds, lions have eagles' heads, the moon is mistakenly colored blood-red, and locusts behave like scorpions. With all the resources at his disposal, I would have expected some more intelligent use of props by the director. The rain of hail and ice mixed with blood served only to alienate the audience.

The seven angels playing on their seven off-key trumpets can scarcely be heard above the thunderclaps in the storming skies and the tumult of the earth's crust being rent asunder below. I could barely hear myself think!

Elsewhere the music is equally shoddy. The lyrics are repetitious ("Holy, holy, holy") and reminiscent to the point of plagiarism of many old church tunes.

The costuming is equally uninspired, with pretty much the entire cast clad in white garments of the most boring variety. Even the heavy, Satan (who appears as anti-Christ), is decked out with what must be the nine millionth set of horns to be put on the Prince of Darkness in the countless little theatre productions of *Devil and Daniel Webster*, and so forth.

Jesus, whose voice was like unto the sound of many waters, was just not in form last night. His speeches were garbled and rushed. The lighting was correspondingly poorly done. His face was so bright I could hardly get a good look at Him.

It seems natural enough that God chose the Root of David, that is, Christ, for the lead role in his final production of the season, because, all nepotism aside, the chip off the Rock of Ages has distinguished himself in several previous features—most notably his role as "the Good Shepherd" in King David's well-received Psalms. In this case, however, as "the Lamb," it was rather sorry miscasting. The irritating peals of thunder and the lackluster landslides that follow the main character around throughout the show seem anything but lamblike.

What it really boils down to is a lack of direction. The choreography is abominable—at one point in chapter six I distinctly saw one-third of the backup multitude tumble into an abyss!

Based on St. John's book Revelations, the Second Coming suffers from lack of subtlety. The recurrent theme of the number seven (seven visions, seven seals, seven churches of Asia, etc.) gets tiresome very quickly—even Doc, Sleepy, and Grumpy couldn't save this bit from its blatantly boring nature.

The Four Horsemen provide some relief in good, solid supporting roles, but the famous ensemble is worked into the show rather awkwardly and their talent is lost in the confusion. Wormword, the falling star which is hitting new lows, gives another cameo appearance that does little to pick up the pace of this anything-but-divine production. Even the popular Michael the Archangel was better in "Genesis" than in this cosmic bomb.

I was also outraged that upon entrance to the show last night I was branded on my forehead with the number 666. A simple ink-stamping of the back of the hand would have saved the management and the public a lot of inconvenience.

Some audience members gnawed their tongues in anguish and cursed the God of Heaven for their pain, and I sympathized completely. It was hot, cacophonous, and quite frankly, not very entertaining.

The Hour of Judgment, if you go, I can guarantee, will be a long one.

Insert Title Here:
A Drama You Supply Yourself

by Mark P. O'Donnell (1975)

The scene: Lord Dessington's well-appointed study. There is a door right leading to the reception room, and a large fireplace whose mantel is cluttered with the paraphernalia of a life spent in the Far East. LORD DESSINGTON enters in a smoking jacket. He is a portly, diffident man, nearing old age. He opens the windows that lead to the terrace and takes a deep breath.

Lord Dessington: An immediately gripping opening line. *(enter LIESL, the maid)*

Liesl: Perfunctory response?

Lord Dessington: Just as good a second line.

Liesl: Whatever comeback you think best.

Lord Dessington: I start to say something when—*(there is a knock on the door)*

Voice *(urgently, outside)*: Rising action!

Lord Dessington: Whatever line you like here.

Liesl: And here.

Lord Dessington: Another line for me.

Liesl: I'll say whatever you wish in this space. *(JAMES MARCH, a young attorney, enters)*

March: Something no doubt rather complicated.

Lord Dessington & Liesl *(together)*: We respond.

March: Further details, probably.

Lord Dessington: More response, if you like.

March: Insert further dialogue here.

Liesl *(after a tense pause)*: Another line. *(DESSINGTON and MARCH* *respond with shock.* LIESL *is led away in handcuffs)* An exit line of some kind or another.

March *(lighting a cigarette)*: I set you up for your last line.

Lord Dessington *(serenely)*: My last line. *(CURTAIN.)*

The Average Guy's Guide to Consciousness Expansion Using Household Objects

by Kurt B. Andersen (1976)

Egg Beater and Soap Bar

An odd combination, you say? Not in the field of altered consciousness, it isn't; here some of the most ordinary household objects can turn out to be valuable tools to the attainment of what some might call Satori, or Nirvana. Mahareshi Tahini Yogi, a relatively obscure Burmese wise man—half talking bear and half baseball catcher—popularized this esoteric meditational method. The meditator simply places a bar of soap (Zest or Dove) on each temple while lying flat on his back, then places the egg beater in his open mouth and begins to "beat." "Very quick indeed," according to the Yogi, "a bubbly white saliva froth emerges from the mouth. Very divine, oh so subtly divine indeed." In layman's terms, the process goes something like this: the frothy spittle cascades down the cheeks, wetting the soap bars and sending a gooey stream of viscous liquid into each ear. "Oh, the soapy spit-stream in the ear is delicately beautiful indeed," says the Yogi. What is the spiritual value of such a technique? An interesting question. But there, my dear reader, you are quite wrong. Only a fool or a half-wit would make such a query in earnest, and of course they often do. But no matter; we shall proceed despite your silly objections.

Microwave Oven and Magnet

Do you happen to have a metal plate embedded in your head? If so, this kinky road to karmic pleasure may be the right path for you.

Developed over a period of several weeks by an enclave of bored San Diego housewives, this method—commonly known as the "Microwave Oven Technique" or more simply the "Modified Microwave Oven Technique"—is considered dangerous by some well-meaning psychiatrists. Warnings about the serious "damage" that the microwave method "may cause" are nonsense, if not indeed different from our own beliefs. In answer to such critics, we may quote a line from Francis Bacon: "Yet notwithstanding as those that first bring honour into their family are commonly more worthy than most that succeed, when not bludgeoned with heavy pebbles." How could one more succinctly or eloquently state the case for "microwave meditation," or even infant lobotomization and genocide?

Since most aspiring truth-seekers with metal plates in their heads are veterans or from upstate New York, this technique is approved for such people and official aid is available under the GI Bill. The process, when gone about correctly, is ridiculously simple: wave a large magnet mysteriously across your scalp and place your entire head on the broiling pan of the microwave oven. Set the oven timer for "Hot Dog and Cold Sandwiches" and you're all set for a visit to the occult world! A Sears Radar-Range will do, although experienced practitioners of the technique prefer the J. C. Penney Infra-Cooker. The choice of oven models is incidental, though, since serious cerebral damage will result using any of them.

Cereal, Garden Hose, and Small Pet

Does a Grape-Nuts enema sound just a little crazy to you? Well, Sufi masters have been making use of this practice for centuries—hundreds of years, in fact—to reach ecstatic states, and cities. It's quite handy to have a partner available to assist the neophyte with this technique, since you'll need both hands free to whip the gerbils with pipe cleaners. Gerbils? Pipe cleaners? *That is correct.* Gerbils, regarded for eons as a sacred symbol of alchemic power, are thought by Sufi masters to provide cosmic aid to those bold enough to abuse the frisky creatures. This particular method of consciousness expansion, called by the Hindu word *Ra-mada*, requires 1) a short length of ordinary garden hose, 2) an ordinary box of Grape-Nuts cereal, 3) an ordinary gerbil, and 4) your child's ordinary Tinker Toy set. Even before you finish reading this article, instruct your meditational "buddy" to prepare the hose and Grape-Nuts. (This will be an anal enema, naturally, in the Dutch fashion.) Your gerbil should be starved for several days before being used as a consciousness-altering device or, alternatively, wrapped in damp cheesecloth and beat senseless with a rubber mallet.

As the crunchy rivulet of Grape-Nuts begins to work its way up your intestine, build a sturdy cagelike structure out of Tinker Toys, just large enough to cover your arm when outstretched. At a moment that seems appropriate, place the gerbil on your arm and quickly entrap him on it with the Tinker Toy cage. (The Grape-Nuts should prove quite irritating by now. Ignore this minor nuisance.) As the dazed little rodent scurries to and fro on your arm, nipping small chunks of soft flesh from your wrist, proceed to whip him mercilessly with an eight-inch pipe cleaner. Very soon, if not before, there will come a point at which you can no longer withstand the extraordinary degree of sensory input: neural circuits "flash" and a sort of heavenly sensation, and perhaps a glimpse into Reality, occurs. (This is what the Sufi masters reluctantly call "Ra-mada In.") You are dumbstruck. You sense an awesome power. You uncomfortable and nauseous. For a moment, you are divine.

Lightbulb, Scotch Tape, and Balloon

Bubba Bomb Dass, the former LSD proponent and Harvard man-about-town, has recently been promoting the efficacy of this peculiar brand of mind-expansion. Now practiced by literally tens of people, the technique is explained by Bomb Dass in his last book, *Be Here As Soon As Is Conveniently Possible.* "When we are one with all, yes, we are one. How may this be so? It simply is, as it must be," writes Bomb Dass. Scotch tape, regarded for centuries as a sacred symbol of alchemic power, is used here to fasten lightbulbs to one's body. It may sound a bit kooky to the uninitiated and narrow-minded, but according to the Master, "Searing, white-hot lightbulbs placed on

the naked body is, where Oneness is the penultimate, divinely won-
derfully delightful. As it pleases you." Inscrutable as it may seem, six
to eight lightbulbs, each attached to an electrical outlet and burning
brightly, are placed against the body and held securely with strips
of Scotch tape. As one might expect, the hot bulbs are irritating at
first, particularly the ones fastened under each thigh. When the pain
becomes a thing of the past, when it has ceased to be simply another
earthly worry, inflate a large, sausage-shaped balloon. Just before the
balloon explodes, roll around slowly on a hard floor, bursting each
lightbulb and sending fiery shards of glass and metal into your skin.
Suddenly, and in a sense unexpectedly, the balloon pops and *voilà*—
Perfect Knowledge, if not serious cuts and second-degree burns,
is yours! "Now what could be simpler than this?" Bomb Dass asks
prospective seekers-of-truth. And, indeed, we posit the same query
to our readers. "Veritas simplicitas" becomes more than a hackneyed
Greek slogan to the followers of this spiritual trail, as you may soon
discover for yourself. God willing.

My Favorite Jokes by God

by Roger Parloff (1976)

EDITOR'S NOTE: God has been delighting generations of believers with His upbeat alternative to amoral egoistic materialism. He is best known for His creation of the world and all its inhabitants from out of nothing, but He has also made quite a name for Himself in the world of humor. The driving force behind *The Divine Comedy*, God is known among His intimates as an Absolute Scream.

When He's not minding the Kingdom of Light, God likes to spend time in ineffable bliss. At such times He is fond of sitting back in His Throne of Glory and spinning yarns with His one true Son, the three Fates, a few cherubic angels, and a host of others.

Here are some of God's favorite jokes:

*   *   *

A bum comes up to me on the street. He says to me, "I haven't had a bite in weeks," so I clothed him and fed him and exalted him.

*   *   *

A guy comes up to me on the street and asks, "Hey, why did the chicken cross the road?" So I says to him, "Where wast thou when I laid the foundations of the earth?"

*   *   *

What an affable guy that archangel Raphael is. The other day he comes up to me and says, "Geez, I just flew in from the coast, and boy, was the plane ride tiresome."

*   *   *

Speaking of angels, have you heard this one?
Q: What do you call a 5,500-year-old fallen angel in the second grade?
A: Gifted.

*   *   *

115

Let's face it. I'm no Norman Niceguy. The other day I slew a man in my infinite wisdom. What he was doing in my infinite wisdom I'll never know.

* * *

When cometh pride *not* before a fall? In the dictionary.

* * *

Who does an Almighty Being afflict with pain and misery? Anybody he wants to.

Excommunication:
And How You Can Avoid It

by Paul S. Redford (1976)

Perhaps you're making the mistake of so many others: thinking "It can't happen to me." And maybe you'll let yourself get a little bit careless. Then one day, seemingly out of the blue, the postman will bring you the tragic news: you've been anathemized by the Holy See. Suddenly you are victim of the tragedy the National Census Bureau estimates strikes on the average .75 American families every three hundred years: excommunication. How does the average citizen cope with such a problem?

One victim of excommunication, Mrs. Martin Luther, remembers vividly the embarrassment and humiliation of the experience:

"I remember when Marty first told me he'd been excommunicated. I didn't even know what the word meant. I mean, I thought it was one of those weird Jewish customs they did with little boys, you know, even though I knew Marty wasn't Jewish. But when he told me it carried with it the imperial ban from Emperor Charles V, then I knew we were in big trouble.

"It wasn't so much me I was worried about—and Marty always had the Reformation to keep his mind off things. It was the kids; you know how rough the peer group can be on a kid whose own father's been denied the rite of Christian burial by the College of Cardinals.

"But thank God, at least we had the support of friends. I don't know how we could have pulled through without Erasmus of Rotterdam, who was a wonderful help. Mrs. Erasmus was always bringing over cookies and casseroles, and they both helped babysit the kids when Marty had to flee to Wartburg to escape the Edict of Worms. We couldn't have made it without them."

Of course the best way to handle excommunication is simply not run the risk of letting it happen to you. When it comes to being execrated by the Vatican, an ounce of prevention is worth a pound of cure! Your local newspaper probably runs a weekly list in the Arts Section of the Index of Prohibited Books; follow it carefully. And to further help you I've compiled, with the friendly advice of Dominican Tomás de Torquemada, Grand Inquisitor of Castile, the following checklist of things that might get you in hot water with the ecclesiastical hierarchy. Tear out this page and keep it in your wallet, and, like thousands of other smart members of the faithful, you too can make sure you'll never have to face the unpleasant shock of a decree of "Decet Romanum ponticen"!

1) *Personal Violence Against the Pope.* This is an easy mistake to make. A pope picks a fight with you in a bar; a pope jumps you in a dark alley—your natural instinct would be to fight back. But this is exactly the wrong thing to do. Just remember the story of Joan of Arc, the Made of Orlon who kicked Pope Eugenius IV in a restaurant during an argument over who would pick up the tab. She wound up being burned at the stake! Of course, she was canonized afterward, but you can't expect to be so lucky.

2) *Joining of Forbidden Secret Societies.* The Church of Satan and the Illuminati are definitely out. The Boy Scouts are okay, and you can be pretty sure there will be no controversy about your local bridge club or bowling team. A good rule of thumb is to avoid any group that practices ritual sacrifices or that has a funny handshake.

3) *Blasphemous Treatment of the Eucharistic Host.* Do not kick it or call it funny names.

4) *Heresy and Schism.* Don't meddle with either of these, even as a hobby. But if you have been accused of one of them, I warn you: chances are you'll be asked to appear before the Holy Inquisition. It will probably be your first time, and, like most people, you'll nat-

urally be a little nervous. Just remember: there's no need to put on a big act; just *be yourself.* Wear a clean suit, and keep in mind those handy "Inquisition ABC's":

A—Answer every question honestly. No fibs allowed before the Holy Inquisition!

B—Be polite.

C—Clean your fingernails beforehand!

Just keep away from the above four and you can't go wrong. And even if you do wind up being excommunicated, take comfort in Mrs. Luther's closing comments:

"Well sure, it was a terrible thing to happen, but you know, I think it brought us closer together as a family. And I mean, thank God, it wasn't anything like a tax audit or one of the kids needing major dental work. Marty, of course, being a monk, at first had a hard time getting work, since he'd been rejected from the bosom of the Church, but he went freelance and things worked out in the end. So it wasn't so bad after all. But we sure will miss the right to receive or dispense holy sacraments."

Rejection Letter

by Ann H. Hodgman (1977)

HARVARD·RADCLIFFE

Committee on Admissions
Byerly Hall, 8 Garden Street
Cambridge, Massachusetts 02138

14 April, 1977

Ms. Brenda Handl
124 Glenroad Rd.
Rochester, NY   14604

Dear Ms. Handl:

I am sorry to inform you that you did not receive any form of
acceptance at Harvard-Radcliffe. While I am, indeed, sorry, as
stated above, I am also glad in a way, for you will now be able
to consider a wide variety of opportunities, ones which it is
very possible you have not considered until this exact instant.
In that way, you should perhaps think of this letter as a "pass-
port" to a new--as yet unchartered--way of life, or sea voyage.

It is not easy for me to have to write this kind of letter, and
I know it must make you very sad, but it is my job. I am not
mean by nature, and I do not wish you to think harshly of me, so
I will give you a little illustration to make my point. Once
there was a young woman (not you) who wished to attend an excellent university, but what she really wanted to do was to get married
and spend all her time entering flower shows. But her grades were
very good, but she took herself too seriously, and didn't shave
her legs, so she was almost admitted, but then at the last minute
she wasn't. Whiff this, "Ms." so-called Handl: it <u>was</u> you! No,
just kidding, no offense. It was in fact someone el<u>se</u>, and in
any case she was admitted.

I hope that my anecdote will increase your sense of penis envy
--whoops! I mean, self-assurance. You should not feel that this
decision in any way reflects on you as a person, or on your abilities or unpleasant skin condition. As you are undoubtedly aware,
many zillions of <u>thoroughly qualified</u> applicants are turned away
each year simply <u>because they are not</u> admitted to Harvard-Radcliffe.
Some of these applicants are famous, too, while others, embittered
by their rejection letters, become cheapened and turn to lives of
crime and deception. Which are you? Only time will tell, but time
heals all wounds: sculpt it into any bandage you choose.

Finally, I would like to suggest that you bracket the above **para**-
graph and leave this letter for your mother to find. I greatly
enjoyed our little chat when she called the Admissions Office a
week or so ago. Good-bye.

Sincerely,

Bob ☺

Robert "The Man" Avery
Director of Admissions

R"M"A:edc
no enclosures

--AHH

I Am Now Aboard the UFO

by David L. Owen (1977)

I am now aboard the UFO. I am dictating the words that you are reading into a tiny tape recorder of earthly manufacture that I was able to conceal in my clothing before I was taken prisoner. (Perhaps I am being unfair to the aliens who now control my destiny; let me change the last clause of the previous sentence to "before I was made the guest of these curious beings from a strange and distant world.")

I feel disoriented. The hands on my wristwatch are moving backward at an extraordinary clip, which suggests that we are traveling through interstellar space, which is to say, that region of space that lies between the stars. At the speed we are traveling, time is distorted and slowed: Although in my last conscious moment on earth the date was early New Year's Day, 1978, it is now August 21, 1947, and eggs are about twenty-five cents a dozen. I have learned from

reading certain documents aboard the UFO that the alien beings who presently have me in their power are capable of traveling faster than the speed of light, but never do, because they are afraid of the dark. Theirs is a sleek craft, not lacking in amenities, but made of metals unknown to men, and fully suited to the rigors of life in distant galaxies.

Common courtesy demands that I describe my captors, or companions, if you will. . . . They are a hardy race from beyond the stars, hundreds and hundreds of miles away; they have no hair to speak of, and their arms—or "appendages"—are covered with ancient inscriptions. They have no legs, but they do wear tiny shoes upon their "fingers," which are actually sensitive electronic probes capable of reading the innermost thoughts of human beings. On the planet where these creatures come from, war is unknown.

What's that? (An alien being is now addressing me in my own language, which is good mongrel English: he is asking me for my wristwatch; this ought to be amusing.) Why, certainly, old boy. Wear it in good health. (He is examining my timepiece with his single pulsating eye. Something seems to displease him. How crude an instrument this "toy" must seem to a being of such vastly superior intelligence!) Never seen anything like it, I imagine. . . . What? What's that? (He is returning my wristwatch to me. He says that he has no use for it, as the hands are running backward. Suddenly, I feel drowsy. . . .)

I am now broad awake and standing in a land too marvelous for speech, too fabulous for comprehension. I have a wife from among the alien race, and two strapping children who resemble me not a little. Our home is modest. An intricate inscription carved upon a perfect diamond the size of the Empire State Building informs me that the name of this planet is "Earth-2."

My new home is nothing like my old. Over there is a mountain taller than Everest, and covered with more snow. Over there is a river longer than the Mississippi. (But no water flows between its banks; the stream is pure mercury.) Over there is a mighty chasm that could contain a thousand earths. And over there is a motion picture screen on which all the movies ever made on earth could be shown at once. But more than all of these marvels, it is the *size* of the things on this planet that astonishes me.

Before me spreads an immense field under cultivation. In some ways the field resembles the rolling farmlands I remember from the days of my youth. But an earthly farmer would feel humbly out of place on these acres, for the "crop" that here is being readied for harvest consists not of familiar vegetables and grains, but of highly advanced technological devices and instruments. On Earth-2, the most marvelous types of machinery grow right out of the ground, attached to the nuturing soil by sturdy vines and stalks, needful of only cursory attention from the "farmers" charged with their care. In the plot nearest me, a vast spaceship that will one day carry my neighbors to a distant galaxy rises gleaming from the topsoil and swells to fruition, as if in anticipation of its maiden flight. This intriguing feature of my adopted environment accounts in many ways for the technological superiority of the alien race, although it also points to one of its limitations: since foodstuffs do not grow naturally from the ground, nutrients must be laboriously synthesized from base elements, and the cultural staple is a dry white paste almost identical in its chemical composition to Cremora. Time, however, has taught me to savor it.

I have learned a great deal on my voyage through time and space. I now know, for instance, that the universe is not, as Einstein speculated, "saddle-shaped": it actually looks like a big bow tie. I have also learned what became of those coded radio messages American scientists used to broadcast into space in the hopes that alien intelligences would intercept them and respond: Huge antennas on this planet have been picking them up for some time. The scientists here don't quite know what to make of the broadcasts, but the teenagers find them very agreeable and occasionally dance to them.

This morning I am to meet the alien chieftain, a very great honor bestowed upon only the most important of dignitaries. I hope that I may prove worthy. I already know a little about the leader: His name is "Big Mike" and he is a cube of metal. I will bring him a message of peace and brotherhood from my native Earth, and I feel certain that he will reciprocate. If he offers me a token of his trust, or a gem the size of my fist, I will accept. Suddenly, I feel drowsy. . . .

I am back on planet Earth, safe and sound. This must be my old neighborhood—I recognize the street signs—but things have changed since I last stood on this spot. My old, rambling house is gone, and in its place stands the "Friendship Hospital and Orphanage for Everyone Regardless of Race, Creed or Color." It is heated by solar energy. On the corner where the local bar once stood is a beautiful church. The stained-glass windows spell out a message: "Peace to All Earthlings from the Strange Creatures in Outer Space P. S.: All Wars Are Canceled." I guess we all have some apologies to make.

Glasses Comix

by Thomas W. Gammill (1978)

A Brief Look at Friendship
Through Your Life

by Kevin P. Curran (1979)

Chapter One—Early Friends, *or* What's a Dickfor?
Childhood pals are the only real friends you'll ever have. Through strange rites involving the flipping of baseball cards, the capturing of fuzzies, and the exchange of your first dirty joke, you acquired pals and palettes (if artistically inclined) who either moved away or became unbearable in the seventh grade. Do not expect them to be helpful to you later on in life. If lucky you might parlay these youthful connections into a series of Chubby Santa Christmas cards from year to year.

Chapter Two—High School
In high school the possibility still exists to have friendship, but it is far more important to be popular. This involves either athletic prowess or large breasts: never the two in combination. In high school sleaze glands begin functioning at an increased rate. In the male they produce large amounts of testosterone, which he may use as hair tonic, if desired. Lunch money may be obtained through the application of sufficient peer pressure, usually judged as enough to wrench an arm from the socket. However, a place in a prestigious Wall Street law firm will forever be denied the user of such limited tactics.

Leisure Time Safety:
Some Do's and Do Not's

by Pamela R. Norris (1979)

Leisure time should be fun time, but you can't take a vacation from safety! Some kinds of accidents are well documented (for example, every elementary school teacher is personally acquainted with one person whose head was knocked off by a passing truck, or one whose face *stuck* that way), but vacation-time hazards are often neglected. "I'm here to have fun," vacationers insist, "not to avoid mutilating myself! It's my *vacation*, for heaven's sakes!" But try to exercise a little caution, and make sure your well-deserved "time off" isn't spoiled by an unplanned and unsightly accident.

Sleeping

Nearly everyone loves to get in some shut-eye in the hours between workdays! Unfortunately, this year alone, hundreds of thousands of people will die in their sleep, accounting for nearly 60 percent of all deaths. But, if you still want to sleep in your free time, take a few simple precautions. **Do** keep your hands and feet inside. **Do not** smoke or smolder in bed. **Do not** have scary dreams or dreams in which you die, because if you die in your dreams you will die for real. **Do not** ask how we can possibly have even the flimsiest reason for thinking this is true.

Reading Books

A book can be a magic express to faraway lands . . . one that can derail at any second, leaving your mangled corpse by the tracks. **Do not** think, "It can't happen to me. Book safety? Who gives three hoots?" This is an extremely dangerous way of thinking. For one thing, if you mutter it aloud, you might be placed in a home.

For another, this who-cares-not-me attitude encourages those speed-readers who are probably "skimming" their way to a handful of paper cuts, hefty library fines, or worse. And anyone who's ever been slammed across the base of the neck with a twelve-pound dictionary doesn't need to tell you to have a healthy respect for books, our potentially dangerous friends.

Listening to Records
This is another popular leisure time activity that can be lots of fun if done safely. **Know in advance** where all exits are. **Do not** play your records at excessive speeds. The momentary thrill of hearing the Lettermen sound like Alvin and the Chipmunks is not worth the risks involved in high-speed accidents. Remain strapped in your chair at all times, unless dancing, in which case you should take care to keep both feet and at least one hand on the floor at all times to avoid a nasty fall.

Watching TV
This seemingly harmless pastime has taken its toll in the last twenty or so years, simply because some people neglect the rules. **Never** watch someone else's TV. (Would you use their toothbrush?!) **Do not** operate the TV without reading the instructions. **Showing off** and watching TV do not mix, and could leave you in a watery grave.

Space: 1984?

by John F. Bowman (1979)

NY, NY (AP) Last night an enormous spacecraft hovered over New York. Suddenly and without warning, it fired lasers at the city beneath, murdering everyone. The flying saucer then returned to its home planet in the Alpha Centauri solar system.

This is a true story. Don't tell me "It's a made-up story," or "It's a funny joke, only you left out the punch line." That would be false. It would also, unfortunately, be highly indicative of a national trend, a general unwillingness to believe in the evils of "outer space." A recent poll in *Mother Earth News* confirms this trend. When asked, "What do you fear most?" 40 percent responded "defoliation due to harmful propellants in the ozone layer," another 40 percent replied "defoliation due to nuclear holocaust," while only 5 percent feared "an attack of scary space creatures who won't hesitate to press their slimy, scale-infested bodies against the tender-yet-firm flesh of our daughters." Don't ask about the other 15 percent. What they said would make your head spin.

I believe I've made my point. A dangerous trend is afoot, a trend that must be arrested at all costs, for I fear for the future of our planet, Earth. Time was that a fellow could hardly say "neptunian" in a crowded bar without some patriotic citizen rushing home and returning with hand grenades and rifles for all. Soon the bar would echo with cries of "I've seen the whites of their eyes!" and the building across the street (rumored to be alien headquarters) would be in a fine fettle by midnight. But times have changed. Today that same citizen would rush home all right, only now he'd return with an autograph book and the keys to the city.

Why the change? Popular movies haven't helped. *Star Wars* portrayed aliens as a friendly lot always willing to lend their brethren a helping hand, even if they looked like some of the nuts in the "barroom" scene. *Close Encounters* was even worse; here, aliens were portrayed as a bunch of big babies, whom anyone could beat up. The media event that most affected changing American perceptions, however, occurred some time ago, and must be explored in further detail.

Picture a playground in the Midwest around the turn of the century. A ten-year-old youth is standing alone, surrounded by his abusive classmates. "Orson is a chub-head! Orson weighs a lot of pounds!" they taunt, and the obese child has no recourse but to grin sheepishly and silently plot the day of his revenge. Twenty years later, that day finally comes.

The scene shifts to New York in 1936. A young man climbs the fire escape of the Mercury Theatre, all the while muttering, "Fattypants, eh? Why, I'll show them!" He spots an open window to Studio C, which is presently broadcasting a program of popular music throughout the world. In a split second he jumps through the open window, grabs an unattended microphone and screams "The Martians have invaded the Earth! Death ray torture abounds in otherworldly reign of terror!" An alert stagehand quickly throws the power switch, but the damage has already been done. All over the Earth, people march to the nearest cliff and make like lemmings, rather than subject themselves to the churlish whims of an alien race. The death toll? Over several thousand men, women, and other men in Montana alone!

By the next day the panic is over, and it seems that everyone feels just a wee bit silly about overreacting to Orson's little prank. "Hey, Charly!" one neighbor greets another. "You sure looked like an idiot running through the streets with a bag over your head and screaming about the Martians in your kitchen!" But Charly isn't about to admit to anything. "Me? You must have me confused with my moron of a wife, who died painfully from self-inflicted gunshot and knife wounds. Me? Believe in Martians? In a pig's eye!" The Depression, Hiroshima, and double-digit inflation soon follow; as a result Americans have all but forgotten about the alien forces mustering *at this very moment* in a crater on the dark side of the moon.

Therefore, I urge all of you to take the following preventive measures—before it's too late. Demand proper identification from your friends and relatives. If they refuse, proceed to fisticuffs. Be sure to carry a gun in your car at all times, for it is more than likely that the "officer" arresting you for a "speeding violation" is in actuality a Pluto scout trying to get a closer look at complex American know-how. Above all else, keep your eyes on the skies. We'll be the first to know.

Double-parked
on Sunset Boulevard

by Andy S. Borowitz (1979)

One night last August I came back from buying some discount cigarettes and found some guys from the collection agency repossessing my apartment. I guess I had some unpaid bills—the only part of my car I had fully financed was the dice—so the big boys from the collection agency had put a regular Skip Tracy on my tail. I knew what they were up to as early as June, when every morning while I was in the shower some wiseguy came in and repossessed the sports section from my *L.A. Times*. Maybe that was their way of telling me to watch my step, I don't know. All I know is that for the entire summer I thought that the Dodgers were still in the pennant race.

I didn't mind it when the bloodhounds started repossessing the furniture or the flatwear or the sports—you figure you can learn to do without. For the entire month of July I ate my dinner right off the floor and tried to approximate the baseball standings by reading the Dow Jones closings and the wedding announcements. But repossessing my apartment was going a little too far, I thought. I saw them remove the hinges from the door and pull the damn thing out of the jamb nonchalantly, as if they were pulling a section out of the newspaper. Then they started scraping off the paint, pulling up the carpet, removing the walls and ceiling. My landlord, a nervous Hawaiian, looked on the whole thing with furrows in his forehead you could file letters in. He'd seen it happen before, he'd see it again, but he kept on worrying. He'd been shell-shocked. Pearl Harbor. A Japanese bomber shot a coconut off a tree and knocked him out with it. To this day he doesn't let you keep plants in his building.

I wasn't going to stick around while the collection weasels were stacking my floor into the back of their van. While they were getting the equipment necessary to repossess my plumbing, I sneaked into the bathroom, now an open-air facility, and nabbed my toothbrush. Then I headed for my car. Nobody, not even this Skip Tracy, was going to get his hands on my car. And if he did, the two thousand dollars' worth of unpaid parking tickets was his problem, not mine.

You may have guessed by now I'm a writer. I figured the story about the Hawaiian would be an easy tip-off, a dead giveaway; the Hawaiian is the kind of thing writers take notice of and write about. When the average guy passes a nervous Hawaiian in the hall, and the Hawaiian is mumbling to himself and shaking so much that his helmet almost flies off, the average guy isn't apt to notice anything out of the ordinary. At the most, he'll say to himself, "What a weirdo," or "What a crummy guy." A writer would notice it and write about it. That's what makes him a writer. I'm not saying I'm a writer like Keats or Sheldon. I don't care if my name isn't on hardcover books with a lot of literary wiseguys' names on them. Who the hell needs that? I don't have to be an alternate selection of the Book-of-the-Month Club to know my writing's good. You see, I get paid money for my writing. Good money. Any writer who says he doesn't want that is either lying or he already has it.

I was doing fine with this writing game for a long time. Then, without any warning, I hit a dry spell. Really dry. I couldn't write the back of a cereal box and sell it. I know that for a fact because both Post and Kellogg's rejected my stuff. I was just a two-bit, second-rate hack screenwriter with a few old ideas, no money, and dwindling flatwear. I needed a break and I needed it bad. I threw my toothbrush in the back seat and headed for Embassy Studios.

A month earlier, I'd given a copy of a treatment I'd written for a proposed screenplay to my old friend Jack Lessing, one of the studio honchos at Embassy. I hadn't heard a word from him—he'd been sitting on the thing as if he were expecting it to hatch. I didn't care if he thought it was good or not, I just needed some dough—a contract, an advance, a kill-fee, even a tip. Dough. Jack gave me an icy reception. He said that the premise of my story was too predictable and hackneyed: the movie was about a man who gets the Midas touch and everything he touches turns into a muffler. Jack said he'd seen the same idea come across his desk five times that month. His assistant and head reader, a frigid-looking creep from Vassar, backed him up. I asked Jack for twenty bucks to put some gas in my tank. He gave me fifteen and I left.

When I got out to my car, I noticed that somebody had torn off the antenna. I thought it might have been an Embassy actor who'd just blown a screen test until I saw the sticker from a collection agency, lying above the open antenna-socket like a sinister eyebrow. Skip was on my trail, all right. As I drove through L.A. looking for gas, I wondered if I was crazy to stay in a game I wasn't winning and was having trouble tying. I could always go back to my old job at the Cincinnati newspaper, writing the farm report five days a week. Five days a week, nine to five, a hundred fifty each Friday, before taxes. No, I wasn't going to give up on Los Angeles yet—not while I had my car, fifteen dollars, and a toothbrush in the back. I had to buy some paste, I remembered.

I tried the other studios, but I guess the last few years hadn't made much of a name for me. The fat cats at Coronet Pictures wouldn't touch me with a ten-foot boom, and the big boy over there, Zach Berman, told me as much. I had a bad brush with Berman a few years earlier over a script I'd written for a movie called *Hemo the Magnificent*. The title really threw me for a loop. I thought they wanted a costume epic, not an educational film on the circulation system. Coronet didn't even give me a kill-fee for my trouble. A few years had gone by, and now Berman wasn't even going to give me the time of day, claiming he'd left his watch on his night-table.

Next I tried Warner Brothers. No work. Nothing. I pressed harder—I'd do anything, rewrites on silent Westerns, anything. My pal at the studio, Hubert Winn, thought he was doing me a big favor when he finally offered me a job writing novelizations of three of the better Looney Tunes. I asked him if I'd get cash up front for doing it, and he nixed me. I told him to go fly a kite and I blew out of his office. Who the hell did he think I was? Outside, someone had stripped off my glove compartment.

I realized I was getting nowhere in Hollywood—Hollywood's really sold out these days, I guess. If Orson Welles walked into RKO today with the script of *Citizen Kane*, they'd probably tell him to go novelize Woody Woodpecker. I ran into my agent, Spats Honey. Spats had read a piece I wrote for *Car and Driver* a few years earlier and thought I was a hot commodity. "Kid," he told me that night in the Kon-Tiki Lounge, "when I read your stuff, my skin breaks out in dollar signs." He took me on. Like me, Spats wasn't too happy about my current dry spell, because it meant that he had to rely less on his income as a literary agent and more on his income as a professional gambler. Unfortunately, Spats, the horses, and I were all having dry spells that summer. So Spats had the sound of urgency in his voice when he told me he had gotten me a little job: some cheesy book publisher in San Diego was putting out a pictorial history book on wax lips, and needed a writer fast. It was the usual deal for that kind of book: I supply the captions and copy, they supply the lips. As Spats and I moved the cartons of historic lips into my car, he told me about another job he'd snagged for me—writing copy for Killer Killjoy, one of Los Angeles's professional wrestlers. I thanked Spats and gave him a dollar fifty. He gets 10 percent of everything I make, no matter how I make it.

The next week I wrote good stuff and got paid for it. A lot of people would say that writing for a professional wrestler like Killjoy was a crass, commercial thing to do, a Hollywood sellout. All right, so Killjoy isn't the best wrestler in the world. He's still damn good at what he does. And I'm damn good at what I do. We're both just doing our job. The crowd went wild every time Killjoy shouted to his opponent, "I will mangle you," a line I penned. So I guess you could say that both Killjoy and I did a pretty professional job.

I had just spent a night writing some threatening slurs against one of Killjoy's upcoming adversaries, Dr. Nannook, when I noticed that somebody had put a blowtorch to the side of my car and pulled off the driver's door. In the front seat, a melted mass of what was once a very important collection of wax lips merged to form one large, mocking grin.

I knew that once the San Diego book publisher found out about the accident, I'd be through on the coast. Spats gave me some advice he picked up from some of his associates: if someone is after you and the heat's on, pack a rod and lie low. I couldn't afford a rod and I was already lying as low as I could without being six feet under. So Spats came up with another plan: he got me a job as a skywriter. Instead of lying low I'd be flying high. The job worked out well for a while, although I was disappointed that the skywriting company refused to pay me by the word. I guess they figured I'd start padding up there and they didn't want me to waste any of their smoke just to pick up a few extra bucks. But what the hell. I was writing, they were paying.

Then it happened. I was in the middle of writing "USE GEM BLADES" over Hollywood when I caught sight of something odd on the ground with a pair of binoculars. *No, it couldn't be,* I thought. I looked again. It was what I thought I saw. Somebody, probably Skip Tracy, had towed my car and it sat, trunkless, double-parked on Sunset Boulevard. That was the last straw. I landed the plane in a back lot at Universal, where they were filming a jungle picture, dodged some natives, and raced to my car. Crashing through the parked car that had hemmed my car in, I did sixty down Sunset Boulevard. Skip Tracy was following me, doing sixty in a cab.

The chase must have gone on long after the cab's meter ran out of digits. Finally, I ditched him through a stroke of luck: the cabbie went off duty. But I still wasn't going to take any chances. As I drove down past the mansions of Sunset Boulevard, I saw one huge house with an empty space in the garage. I knew from the moment I saw the space that this would be my big break—I could hide my car there until the heat on my tail cooled off a little. When I got out of my car, I heard a strange voice next to me:

"Madame has been waiting for you."

I turned around and saw a butler wearing a chauffeur's cap who looked like he'd gone to charm school with Bela Lugosi. He spoke again.

"Madame Garbo has been waiting for you. Please do come in."

The name rang a bell. I looked around the place.

"No, thanks," I told the formal zombie. "Get me out of this creep joint," I told myself.

Last week I got my old job back in Cincinnati.

Lovers Once

by Mark A. Doyle (1979)

I first saw him in the soda fountain. Not actually in the fountain—
there's no real fountain to be in. Rather, he was sitting at one of
the small tables with a big sundae. He had the table tilted toward
himself, in a cute kind of way, and he was watching the sundae
slide down the table and into his lap. After seeing the big dish of
ice cream take three plunges onto his shirt, I made my advance to
his table.

"What are you doing?" I asked.

He looked up and after a second said, "Dropping ice cream into
my lap like a moron." I knew I would like him.

"Are you a moron?" I asked.

"Hey, wait a minute. One question at a time," he said with suspicion. Then he answered, "It looks that way."

"What a guy," I thought to myself. Then out loud, "Do you want
to go steady with me?" He considered the chocolate sauce on his
belt, he considered the wet pool collecting in his seat, then he considered the proposition.

"Will I be able to get out of this chair?"

"Sure."

"Okay then."

He got up from the table and I took his hand on the way out.
"Call me Jim," he said.

"Call me a lucky girl," I replied as he walked into the glass door.
What a doll.

I saw him again the next night. He was driving over to the house
and we were going out on a date. He was on time, but he missed
the driveway and put the car on the front lawn. He walked to the
door, hands thrust nervously into his pockets, and I invited him in
to meet my parents. When he reached to shake my father's hand,

his pants dropped to his ankles. "He's a comedian on top of it all," I thought. A classic meet-the-parents ploy, perfect for breaking the ice. I walked out the door aglow.

We went to a party just down the street. I found my friends and started talking with them; Jim took up right away with the dog. They were really entertaining each other. He was fine until I saw him remove someone, politely, from an easy chair. He told the dog to sit and then picked up the chair and carried it to the other side of the room. Then he ran back to the dog and commanded, "Okay, fetch!" The dog got up and walked away.

"I'd better get him before he finds the ice cream," I told my friends and then excused myself.

I called him the next day with the bad news. "Jim, we have to break up." He didn't say anything. "My dad thinks you're a moron."

"Okay," he said.

We hung up and I cried for a while. I thought back to all the good times we had had. Parents can be so feelingless. Don't they understand? But how could they? I doubt even Jim would understand.

Spooky Magic

by Mike L. Reiss and Al E. Jean (1979)

Tricks Are for Kids if You Know the Secret

TRICK 1. *The Phantom Face*

EFFECT: The magician covers his face with a borrowed handkerchief. When he whisks it away, his face is completely different.

HOW IT IS DONE: As the handkerchief is placed upon his face, the magician entertains his audience with snappy patter, jokes, and light conversation. After four to five days of this, he removes the handkerchief, revealing a full beard that was not there before. When the audience has stopped applauding, the magician shaves off the beard to prove that it was him all along. Warning: do not attempt this trick if you are a girl.

HINT: A good magician never reveals his secrets.

TRICK 2. *A Scary Card Trick*

EFFECT: A card is removed from the deck and then replaced. The cards are shuffled, and the magician pulls the identical card from the deck.

HOW IT IS DONE: As the magician shuffles the deck, he says, "This trick is so easy that my assistant could do it," and hands the deck to his assistant. The surprised assistant then attempts to perform the trick. If he succeeds, the magician takes credit for a trick well done. If he fails, the magician makes jokes at the assistant's expense, saying, "Ho, ho, my assistant is very stupid. He is retarded."

HINT: A good magician gets paid in advance.

TRICK 3. *A Real Shocker*

EFFECT: The magician walks up to a random member of the

audience and produces from behind his ear a bouquet of colorful flowers.

HOW IT IS DONE: The "random" member of the audience is in actuality a freak with very big ears. Before the show, the magician hides a bouquet of flowers behind one of these big ears.

HINT: A good magician always takes advantage of grotesquely deformed freaks.

TRICK 4. *The Mysterious Balloons*

EFFECT: One minute, the audience sits in an empty room. The next minute, the room is filled with lots of colorful balloons!

HOW IT IS DONE: The magician begins the trick with an open tank of ether beneath his magician's table. He entertains the audience until, one by one, everybody passes out. To keep from passing out himself, he wears a magician's gas mask. If anyone asks why he does this, the magician jokes: "Ho, ho, my assistant smells very bad. He smells like fish." While the audience sleeps, the magician fills the room with balloons, and then opens the windows to air everything out. The audience will be really surprised upon awakening.

TRICK 5. *Another Scary Card Trick*

EFFECT: A member of the audience thinks of a card. Like magic, every card in the deck becomes that card.

HOW IT IS DONE: The magician walks onstage carrying a white cane and wearing dark glasses, pretending to be blind. He performs this trick, and of course, fails. The audience, however, will be too embarrassed to say this and will applaud politely. Audiences are always nice to blind people.

HINT: A good magician will buy this book and urge his friends to do the same.

TRICK 6. *The Vanishing Assistant*

EFFECT: The magician's assistant is handcuffed, doused with kerosene, set afire, and thrown in a sealed tank of water. The tank is covered. Within seconds, the assistant appears, dry and unharmed.

HOW IT IS DONE: It is not the assistant who returns, but actually his identical twin brother.

HINT: A good magician has an alibi for the time of murder.

A Cover from 1980

Cover by John D. Brancato

A Call for Subscribers

(1981)

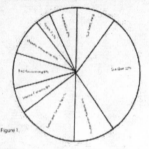
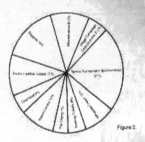

Toys Make War Child's Play

by Patric M. Verrone and Mike L. Reiss (1981)

"Girl Killed in Barbie Doll Explosion." "Two Maimed in Play-Doh Fun Factory Accident." "Child Chokes to Death on Easy Bake Oven." "Five Injured in Freak Slinky Fire." The number of children hurt, crippled, or killed each year by defective toys is hardly funny. But someday, the negative qualities of these lethal playthings may be put to good use. That someday is today.

After the devastation of a small Midwestern town following the explosion of a Close 'N Play left out in the rain, the Defense Department began to take notice. Perhaps these toys of terror could be put to use in warfare as obliterative weaponry. As one general expressed it, "Let *their* kids get mangled for a change." Top-secret research in the field of fun armaments has shown that toys are deadlier, more reliable, and, except for batteries, cheaper than conventional weapons. The results of this research are here released to the public for the first time:

This campsite is constructed completely of Lego blocks and can be disassembled within minutes. Greater mobility is afforded by the handy carrying case.

The Etch-A-Sketch—This budding artist's tool has long been criticized because of the extreme fragility of the cover glass and the mysterious silver substance within (the manufacturers, Ohio Art, are themselves unsure of its composition, though trace amounts of strontium and other radioactive wastes have been detected). These devices have made conventional landmines obsolete: lying flush with the ground, when stepped upon, the glass shatters, the shards lacerating the boot, sock, and foot of the victim; then the silver is released into the bloodstream, causing death within seconds. Already, hundreds of these dangerous doodlers have been planted throughout Southeast Asia and Northern Ontario.

Superball—Fortified, enriched, and enlarged, the Superball has become one of the world's most effective projectiles. Fired from a mortar into an open window, the new Supercannonball will carom destructively and indefinitely, gutting the interior of a building while leaving the facade unscathed.

Space Toys—These scaled-down replicas of space weapons prove quite destructive when scaled back up to size. A *Battlestar Galactica* Decapitoy Rocket, fifteen feet in length, can render a platoon headless in a single swipe. The *Star Wars* Marble Death Ray, with minor modifications, at a distance of six miles can put out someone's eye or make him trip; he could break his neck, for cryin' out loud.

This Creepy Crawler maker produced nearly 10,000 rubbery bugs in 1969: these were dropped on a North Vietnamese village.

Teddy Bears—This cuddly suffocant of infants has been adapted for killing on a larger scale. Building-size teddy bears have been constructed, ready for use at a moment's notice. Dropped on a major population center, the fuzzy bruins could flatten buildings and suffocate thousands. The eyes, held in by tree-length spikes, eject on impact, posing great peril. Further danger of

A new resilient polymer in Super Elastic Bubble Plastic produces a nearly impenetrable sheath. Fired from enormous air cannons, the plastic can protectively envelop whole cities within seconds.

asphyxiation can come when the plastic bag the bear came in is also dropped.

Advances in many other areas of toy warfare have been achieved. Novelty straw finger tubes have proved to be an effective substitute for bulkier, more expensive manacles. Silly Putty has replaced microfilm cameras used in espionage for reproducing secret documents. And dressing POWs in a particularly non-flame-retardant brand of children's sleepwear can eliminate the need for any other restraint. Said one MP, "With them things on, those boys is afraid to budge an inch."

Women and Liquor:
The True Story

by Pamela R. Norris (1979)

It's time somebody popped the cork out of these myths about women and drinking. Women alcoholics have had it pretty rough. They're usually portrayed as pathetic housewives in ratty bathrobes knocking back a few at the kitchen sink after Dad and the kids have split, or some aging, over-made-up socialite in a caftan wafting her way through the house in search of some brown liquor. These stereotypes are absurd. Today's female alcoholic is very likely to be a young, dynamic girl-on-the-go, forging her way through the worlds of big business and high finance, her secret alcoholism identifiable only by her ratty bathrobe and the glass in her hand. The woman problem drinker is everywhere; in fact, over 90 percent of all women in the world want nothing more from life than a bottle and a clean glass with some ice. Hard to believe? Think about all the "sexist" stereotypes. Women giggle. Woman say stupid things. Women are uncoordinated at sports. Women are terrible drivers. Now think about how you act when you've had a few too many. Starting to get the picture? It's about time.

Whenever men are spouting off about women, they always ask, "If women are so smart, where are all the women (novelists/politicians/athletes/scientists)?" Clearly, we've had more interesting things to do. While Jerry Ford was pressing the flesh, Betty was bending the elbow. Joe DiMaggio knocked them over the fence, but it was Marilyn who was under the table. And who do women admire more? You tell me. We're all drunks, even your mother. I don't know how much plainer I can put this. Perhaps in dictionary form.

What we say	What it means
women's problems	hangover
check the roast	have a belt
nervous habits	delirium tremens
powder my nose	toss one down
having a migraine	getting ready to pass out
check the baby	pour myself a big one
clean the oven	drink myself silly
nap	alcoholic coma
bridge club	AA
burned myself on the stove	lit myself on fire while rip-roaring

TV: Harmful, or Just Deadly?

by Susan Stevenson Borowitz (1980)

How many times have I witnessed parents passing around photos and talking endlessly about their kids? "My son's the idiot of his class." "Mine's a real palsy. Can't even walk upright." "Today my daughter's teacher called me just to tell me he hates her." "My kid killed someone last week." It makes me wonder about what kind of parents they are, especially when they say, "I don't drink, smoke, or swear. Goddammit, I left my cigarettes at the bar!" Now, how are we supposed to believe them when they lie to us so blatantly, and so ineptly too?

Kids learn from two different sources: their eyes and their ears. Without the one, the other is useless. Yet they are both being ruined by famine, pollution, war, and a lack of attention span. And who do you think is responsible? Our "friend," the television set.

It's about time for our community to wake up and see that TV is nothing but a Pandora's box, with a Pandora's picture tube inside. Take, for instance, the unprecedented growth of juvenile violence. How can parents rear their children to be the docile creatures they should be when the evil presence of TV lurks in the house? Well, they can't. Just looking at a television set can give an impressionable child ideas, and sure enough, he soon realizes that it can be used as a weapon, and then throws it at the first person who hurts his feelings, which is usually me. What's more, it destroys the mind and body of every American child. Kids are very confused when first meeting Mickey Mouse because "television" lures them into believing that the mouse is much smaller. No doubt about it, TV is a danger. It is programmed to harm the youth of this great nation. For instance, turning channels is much like dialing too many phone numbers—their small digits cannot handle the stress. Now, I wouldn't let my kids watch a telephone all day, so why should I let them watch TV?

If the parents of this US of A would sit down and take a look at TV, they would realize what is happening to their youngsters. Too many "educational" shows mold our children into the crooks and jerks they are today. Shows like *Kill Your Mother, Take All the Money from Your Father's Wallet,* and *Please Don't Learn to Spell* cannot help but have a bad influence on our youth, or anyone else's youth. They also offend me, personally. We all know that too many commercials spoil the broth, and by extension, a child's mind as well. Kids see maybe a zillion commercials in one night, and then they bug me to buy them *everything*—Big Wheels, Cheating-Barbies, Biz Bags, and a Hartz two-in-one flea and tick collar. There ought to be a law.

Here we have a child who sits too close to his TV set.

You may realize by now that I don't like television, even though the children do. It hurts them and makes them say really stupid things. My views may be shocking, but at least they're right! I'm just glad there's one person (me) who has the courage to say something about it. We can all agree that TV sets should be used for bookcases instead, bookcases with spelling books inside. There are too many kids who can't spell the simplest of words. If you ask them what C-A-T spells they probably will answer "Shut up." Everyone knows it actually spells "cat"!

The Painter
Who Cut Off His Ear

by Shannon C. Gaughan (1981)

The place of Vincent van Gogh in the Who's Who of paint-
ers' heaven has long been assured. He truly was one of the best
drawers ever—certainly in the Dutch language. And by the way, he
cut off his ear. Deny it if you want, but frankly, Van Gogh's hard-won
popularity never transcends mere curiosity about "the painter who cut
off his ear." Here's proof. Next time you go to a Van Gogh exhibition
look around. What do you see? The kind of people who gather at car
accidents. Then wonder about yourself. Stop wondering. Your presence states, "I like my fine arts with bloody bandages, please."

The following thoughts and reminiscences on Van Gogh should
help to explain what drove the brilliant brush-master to rearrange
his own face. Perhaps once we're all satisfied as to what compelled
the crazy idiot, we just might be able to take a look-see at some of
his paintings. Hmmm? If that's not too much to ask.

Gauguin on Vincent

Oh yeah, thin guy, one ear. No, I remember telling him, "Look, Vinnie, love the stars, love the cypress trees, love the wheatfields. But
you're going nowhere unless you add a few brown-skinned babes."
But Vinnie wouldn't listen to reason. Could've been he couldn't
because of that one ear look he went on with. I knew that would
never catch on. You lose your beret. Beats me why he did a thing
like that in the first place.

My Brother Vincent by Theo van Gogh

I understand completely why he did it. Our parents also gave me
a real homo-type name, and it nearly drove me out too. You see,

everybody thought Vincent was a hairdresser. He really hated that. Finally, one night at this snooty cocktail party, Vincent began to discuss his use of color. Some lady asked him if he thought she should go blond. I saw his eyes go a little screwy. Then she asked if he would cut her hair. So he whipped out his scissors and proved that he was a real butcher when it came to lopping locks. Anybody would've done it.

The writer thinks the self-mutilation was done out of embarrassment. As the self-portrait plainly shows, his ears were too big.

Vincent and Aesthetics by Van Dyke

Although nation-mates, Van Gogh and I differed greatly on the question of aesthetics. Vince was always sort of a crazy guy and well one day . . . I mean, I've always loved a good slapstick routine. Boy oh boy, do I ever. Well, that gross-me-out humor just leaves me cold. Aw, doggonit, Laura, you know what I mean—the ear business. Sure I slammed my fingers in the desk drawer for a laugh, but everybody knew I wasn't really in pain. Yeah, I know I used to fall down a lot as kinduva cute gag, but aw, c'mon now, you guys, you knew I was okay all along, didnya? Gee, I don't know why he'd do a thing like that, buddy, do you? Hey, maybe Allen chewed it off.

My Brother-in-Law Vincent by Mrs. Theo van Gogh

"Inside He Was Just a Little Boy"

First he was supposed to get in at ten o'clock. Then it was eleven. Then it was twelve. By the time it was twelve-thirty my dinner was cold. I was exhausted and I told Theo that I didn't care if I never met his crazy brother. It was especially irritating because I could've used a wash and a set. Probably he lost the ear playing with his army knife.

More Dope on the Ear

It is not known just what Ursula did to provoke Van Gogh to send her his ear. However, the fact that she was a difficult wench is revealed in her letter of reply (printed below), recently found with a pack of what the critics call Van Gogh's "take a powder" letters. At any rate, we're all really mad at her for what she did to Vincent. She really hurt him a lot.

Dear Vincent,

I opened your package this morning. It certainly was an earful! Now listen up, you sicko. If you ever darken my doorway again, I'll toss you out on your ear. As a matter of fact, I've already placed it on my driveway for that exact purpose. Furthermore, I want you to know that from now on I'll be tossing anyone who bothers me out on your ear. Go paint some wavy lines.

I'm all ears,
Ursula

Shortly thereafter Van Gogh entered the mental hospital in Arles. Two years later he shot himself. It would have been nice to be able to say that the world lost a great and noble painter. However, Vincent blew this when he left behind the following suicide note: "I cannot live without Art." So he was a homo after all, and more than likely, a hairdresser too.

Spareribs for Breakfast:
A Story with Lots of Symbolism

by Ken C. Keeler (1981)

It was dark in America that night. Young toughs roamed the street, but, since it was dark, they kept bumping into each other.

In a small log cabin on 14th Street, a family was eating breakfast, but, since it was dark, it was not a pretty sight, or, rather, it would not have been a pretty sight had there beeen enough light by which to see it.

"Mother," said Jim, whose name was short for Jim Makepeace Thackeray, "why does the urban corporate infrastructure hate us so much?"

His mother did not answer immediately. She was a proud woman; while the family was very, very poor, not one of her three children was anything but an American.

"I don't know, Jim," she said finally. "Perhaps it's because we know how to eat breakfast. In the dark."

A police car raced by the cabin, and in the glare of the rotating lights the family gobbled down all the food they could get their hands on. Light makes eating a much more efficient process.

"You know, Mother," said Jim (an American name), philosophically, "sometimes I feel like bottled fabric softener. You find me only in America."

"And England," said his sister Minerva. "Actually, most countries in Western Europe—"

"Get a job, son," said Mr. Makepeace Thackeray, Jim's father, who had left America six years before and had never returned, two pieces of information that, when taken together, make the event just described fairly unlikely.

The rats were out in force as Jim (an American name) left the log cabin on 14th Street. One stopped him and asked for a light. They struck a match and a friendship and walked in pairs to the meat-packing plant. The rat worked on the vermin staff at the plant, a mute commentary on the poor health standards in the American meat-packaging industry. Darkness.

"You being on the vermin staff," said Jim, "I guess we're on opposite sides from now on."

"Not if you don't get the job," replied the rat.

"Don't be optimistic."

It was still dark when Jim was ushered into the head butcher's office. "Know why they call me the head butcher, son?"

"Because your name is Head Butcherson?" ventured Jim.

"Guess again, smarty-pants."

"Because you run the place?" he tried again.

"Say, you're pretty smart, considering I can't see you in this eternal darkness. Let's have a drink."

"No, thanks. Liquor is un-American. You know, there are large rats around here. Isn't that a mute commentary on poor health standards?"

"No; we get them drunk and convince them they're from Panama. Liquor will do that to you, you know. Then we have them deported for un-Americanness."

"It's a rough life."

"Especially in the dark."

It was dark in America that morning as Jim walked home. On the way the sun rose, but it was still dark. The sun shines differently in America; there it is forever dark.

Products . . . for the Tough

by Steve E. Young (1981)

The Tough Company, Inc., is proud to offer these exclusive products for our tough patrons. Not for everyone, these products will brand you (often for life!) as a person willing and able to go beyond the normal boundaries of daring and endurance. Happy shopping!

Sandblasting Shower Head. Shower the natural, wild way, with high pressure abrasives that carve off the most stubborn soil. Comes with air compressor, 50 lbs. sand (reusable). $38.00

Outlet Tester. Is that outlet live? Find out quickly with this handy kit. Includes uninsulated copper wire, instruction booklet. $.27

Lightning Rod Golf Hat. Sure, golf is kind of a sissy sport, but this little gadget will put some real-life danger into your game. Specify color, antenna alloy. $27.00

Shock Amplifiers. Now you can have the ride and handling of an old pickup truck even if you order a modern sedan. Sturdy iron. Order a set for every vehicle in the family. Set of 4: $38.00

Tattoo Kit. Now you can look just as tough as the next guy, at a fraction of the price. Kit includes food coloring, X-Acto knife, instructions. $38.27

Dented Canned Goods Bonanza. We just received a giant shipment. Some are very old. These coveted treats will disappear fast, so order now. $.27 ea.

Insta-Release Lawnmower Blade. With the flick of a switch, this highly tempered blade detaches and cuts an instant swath of destruction in any direction it damn well pleases. Unpredictable fun. $380.00

Sweat Soap. For those embarrassing times when you've been sedentary and cool all day, but still want to smell like a real guy. Comes plain or with mixed-in dirt. $3.80

Steel Tongue Bar. A convenient way to find out how cold those winter days are. Touch the bar with the tip of your tongue when you first go out in the morning. Mounting bracket included. $38.00

Glass Grinder. Don't throw out those old bottles, jars, lightbulbs! Put them through this grinder and add to soups, salads, etc. Comes with three attachments: chunk, chip, dust. $38.00

Aerosol Can Incinerator. Never mind what they say—this is the only way to get rid of those old cans. Comes with heating element, observation port. Puncturing tool optional. $270.00

Super Tanning Lens. Get a darker, quicker tan with this umbrella-size magnifying lens. Set it up, adjust the focal point, and sit back and relax. $270.00

Headless Thumbtacks. Compact, unobtrusive. Harder to use than normal ones. Package of fifty. $2.70

Free with every order of $10 or more: *Stare at the Sun*, by Bernie Retna. This popular book tells how to get the most out of prolonged sun-gazing. How to get started, what to look for, more. 64 pages. Braille key included.

Help Me

by Mark J. Driscoll (1981)

I need money, but fast.

Look, you've got to help me. I need—look, what I mean is, I have a problem. I need money now. I know it sounds crazy, but, well—I'm a used car trapped inside a man's body. I want an operation. Don't laugh at me. Look, don't laugh at me! I'll run you over in a second, smartass.—Sorry. I'm sorry—there I go. Christ. This is just awful. I tried to beat a tollbooth last week and they just laughed at me—said I was crazy. Ha!! Crazy, they call me—sure, I'm crazy.

Crazy in love am I . . .

Aughhh! Shut up. Okay, so I'll tell you the whole story. Billie Holiday is trapped inside of the used car that's trapped inside my body. It's true. *Please*, show some sympathy. Gimme a break! And a new transmission. And patch up this radiator; I'll be ready to go in no time. In fact, for only a few dollars each month, you can release me in my automotive state from the limitations of this human body. Or you can turn the page. Or if you are paralyzed, you can have someone turn the page for you. But at least wait until you get to the end of it.

You really must help—this is driving me mad. Vrooooooooom . . . Sorry, I had to pull away from that awful pun. Aughhh! Help me! Help me get this Pikes Peak sticker off my forehead. Where to turn? Exit 27, then half a mile past the red and white fruit stand and left at the second set of lights. Shut up. Look out! Goddamn Sunday driver . . .

Please give me some help. Give me some hope.

And gimme a pigfoot,
and a bottle of beer

Shut up, Billie. I'm telling you, I'm at my wit's end, and it's not all that it's cracked up to be—everything closes down so early. If you think this piece is running out of gas, you should check the oil and water. Look, don't call the police, okay? I still can't sit down since they tried to tow me the other day. And I haven't broken any law, just this damn gasket, which shouldn't be too much to replace. I need a drink, I feel all light-headed and unleaded. Why are you looking at me like that? Stop it, would you please? Stop it. Stop. Stop!! It's a red light, you idiot! Who you callin' an idiot, you sweet rascal you? Billie, please. This was confusing enough with just two characters. Will they wash my windows, please? Who—

My man, I love him so,
He'll never know.

Billie, stop it. Please help me. I'm trapped in a story that began nowhere and got lost. Pull over to this gas station and see if the guy can tell us where we are.

Illustration by Mel J. Horan

Cry for the Triceratops

by John P. Ziaukas (1981)

I f you think that being a dinosaur is easy, friend, then you are very sadly mistaken. Their lives are potpourris of difficulty from their inception. What with small, warm-blooded, furry creatures—i.e. mammals, e.g. you!—homo sapiens, rummaging through their nests, the modern dinosaur is born into the world largely by tears. And also brontoburgers are another reason.

The young dinosaur contends with problems the average man never sees. Kindergartens place great emphasis on finger-painting, yet the young dinosaur has no fingers. Let alone fit into a child-size desk. His strange looks prompt his playmates to mock him; what with huge rolls of blubber, four legs, and a tail that makes people stand up and take notice, the modern young dinosaur attracts unwanted attention. If his wishes were discerned, he would say, "No thank you," should it be offered. Of course, with his walnut-size brain, today's dinosaur finds rough sailing in the academic seas of primary school, and is often consigned to the remedial group, if not kept back for a year. His teachers invariably remark, "Why, Mrs. Dinosaur, your son is obstreperous. [This is a teacher word, so look it up.] He does not like milk and cookies. He would rather eat banana trees."

When the dinosaur of today feels the first stirrings of embryonic manhood, his social troubles assume new and more terrifying dimensions. Let's face it, pubescence is a traumatic time for most of us (this correspondent excepted), and for dinosaurs, the phase is scarier, in keeping with their immense blubber. What young teen of today would accept a date with a triceratops? Not many, I'll be bound. In most states, dinosaurs may not be issued driver's licenses, so they are left to make their own fun at home with their dates. When dinosaurs sit around the house, they really sit *around* the house, no joke. It should be remembered that this is serious business.

161

The mature dinosaur is battle-scarred, weary, and cynical, but spunky. Bathtubs are poor excuses for semitropical lagoons, so the modern dinosaur must do without or move to Gilligan's or Fantasy Islands. And brontoburgers as well. He otherwise contents himself in using foot power to go to museums of natural history where he can relive old times and shed a tear for lost friends. On his way to the museum, he is likely to run over cars, because city sidewalks were not built to be wide enough for dinosaurs. Even people movers.

The dinosaur is not without pleasures in his largely humdrum life. Having a second brain in his tail makes for rich cocktail party conversation, and his naturally armor-plated head makes him a highly sought after item in college athlete team offices. If we couple this with his naturally perky disposition, we find that the postmodernist dinosaur *can* find succor in life.

Perhaps the most pleasurable pastime for this creature, this *joie de vivre*, this *fil du printemps*, this dinosaur, or call him what you will, is watching the madcap antics of the various dinosaurs on *The Flintstones*. An especial favorite is "Dino"—his name means "the Fatuous One" in the dinosaur tongue. Dinosaurs also take great pleasure in Fred's novel use of his feet to power the family car, instead of using gasoline, which the perceptive reader will discern is made from dinosaurs. Complete integration into the society, as airplanes, construction cranes, and time clocks, makes this past Golden Age—strangely enough—a still-unmet and worthy goal for the dinosaur of today.

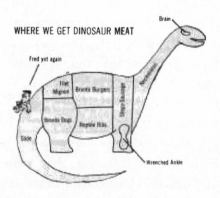

WHERE WE GET DINOSAUR MEAT

Fake Ads

(1981)

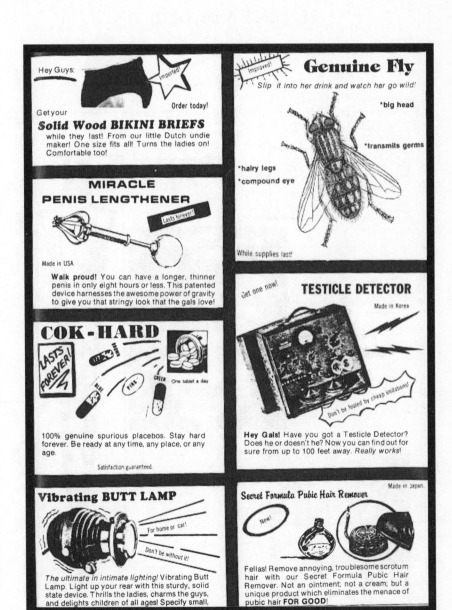

Report for Mr. Zeebok's Archaeology Class

by Steve E. Young (1982)

Report for Mr. Zeebok's Archaeology Class

We already knew that our Lincoln High School was built on the site of an older high school, which in turn replaced the one built when the area was still wilderness. But we didn't know until we started digging that there have been high schools here since the dawn of time! Here are some of the things we found:

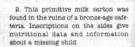

1. Bathroom graffiti seems to be a feature of every age. This example from the Late Classic period includes typical obscenities about unpopular teachers and students.

2. This primitive milk carton was found in the ruins of a bronze-age cafeteria. Inscriptions on the sides give nutritional data and information about a missing child.

3. These impressive Homecoming Parade floats, excavated near our football field, show that the Lincoln students of long ago had plenty of "school spirit."

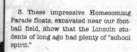

4. The earliest switchblades were actually just plain knives that did not pop open at all. Found in a gym locker of the Homeric period, this example was confiscated by our principal shortly after we dug it up.

SEY

164

Life o' the Party

by Maiya M. Williams (1984)

Everyone knows a Ralph Rummy. You see him at every party, every picnic, every Saturday night at the Bowl-O-Matic. He imbibes a wee more alcohol than he can handle and then becomes unruly and uncontrollable. He makes lewd remarks; staggers from one garbage can to the next ralphing up his lunch from three weeks hence; and then finally, under the mild protests of his friends, he climbs behind the wheel of an automobile and backs slowly over a small child. After the party's over, the picnic is packed up, and the bowling shoes are back on the rack, everyone comes to the mutual agreement that, in the light of day, Ralph Rummy just wasn't much of a fun drunk.

Alcoholism. It's an ugly word; it breaks up families, it destroys careers, it kills. But it also provides a cornucopia of the best live entertainment. Just think how many of the finest, most magical moments of the cinema emanated from the slurred speech of W. C. Fields. Fields: You're ugly! Woman: (disdainfully) You're drunk! Fields: Madam, that may be true, but in the morning, I'll be sober. Surrounding Crowd: Touché! Touché! What a burn!

Even behind the scenes W. C. Fields provided moments of inebriated merriment. Fields: (to bartender) I'd like a whiskey, straight up. Woman: (sitting on a nearby stool) You're nothing but a fat boozehound, not funny at all. Fields: Lady, blow me. Chorus of Drunks: Bravissimo! Atta boy! Our hero!

Many might assess Fields's retort as merely rude, instead of seeing him for the whimsical soak that he is. The distinction, however, is important. It spells the difference between permanent ostracization or an invitation to paradise. Who wants to be around the depressing sort of drunk with a season pass to Alcoholics Anonymous? Well, nobody. The life of a fun drunk is very different. Many find alcohol to be a great boon. Rather than lose their jobs, they find the invitations to entertain at children's birthday parties never stop. Or, if they're lucky, they become well-paid game show hosts.

The society of daffy dipsomaniacs is not open to any old stumblebum. There are specific rules of etiquette that must be followed if one is to truly adopt the title of Fundrunk. Let's follow Farley Fundrunk through a typical cocktail party to pick up a few pointers, shall we?

As all fun drunks have learned, there is nothing more annoying than arriving at a party, throwing back a good deal of rotgut, and then discovering that the host owns none of the accoutrements that really make a party fly. Here we see Farley has come prepared with lampshade, cigars, wacky tie, and a woman's brassiere in his briefcase, should things get really hot. The guests are relieved he has finally arrived and are anticipating the excitement to come.

Once inside, Farley finds that he is quite thirsty for liquor drinks. Since he knows that he is going to visit the bar quite often, he notes the objects in the room that will serve as landmarks to help him make his way once his eyes have clouded and his legs have turned to warm porridge. Farley seems to have marked another path as well, which he plans to use during the evening. You might want to do the same.

Uh-oh, it looks like Farley has had "one too many." Nothing ends a party quite like vomit. The less of it, the better. Again, Farley has come prepared. By establishing a certain room in the house as the Vomitorium with this smart but simple sign, he has saved his host the anguish of discovering "hidden accidents" a month later in some hidden corner of the house. And what fun! What might have been a disgusting faux pas has been transformed into an ancient bacchanalian rite!

Who's the life o' the party? Well, there's no mistaking here. Once revved up for the evening, Farley Fundrunk capers about, urinating in the pool, going for a spin in the clothes dryer, and biting the head off the canary. The height of the evening is always when a prudish matron suddenly cries, "My panty hose—it's gone!" and everyone knows where to find them. "Look! Farley's got *donkey ears*!"

Well, it's time to go home, but not before thanking the host and hostess for a marvelous bar. Don't forget, they have a lot to thank you for. After all, if it weren't for your wild antics, the party might have reverted into a sleep-a-thon. So give them each a great big sloppy lick—hey, you're drunk! You can do anything and get away with it. Even Lady Law turns her head if you can be witty enough. Try these out on the next police officer who pulls you over for drunk driving.

"*Weaving?!?* I was dodging the pink elephants!"

"I know I was speeding, Officer, but my foot felt like fudge and I couldn't find the accelerator. I mean brake. Oh, I don't know what I mean. Windshield wipers. What the hell's the difference? Am I right? Am I right?"

"It's not as bad as it could be, Officer. I'm so cockeyed right now, I thought I hit two ladies instead of just one."

Every party must come to a close, and unfortunately, it often closes with a hangover . . . What am I saying?!? The party *never* stops for the fun drunk. Take one final tip from Farley:

> *When making toasts just raise your glass*
> *And toss it down the hatch*
> *But after ten or twelve of these*
> *Beware the lighted match!*

A Weekend in the Country:
Esquire's Guide to Practical Packing

by Richard J. Appel (1984)

How many times have you had a conversation that goes something like this:

Friend 1 (*with good cheer*): Hey, let's go away for the weekend.
Friend 2: Sounds like a great idea.
Friend 3: What fun.
Friend 4: Count me in.
Friend 5: Me too! Just give me five days to pack . . .
Friends 1–4: Ah, well, actually, this weekend doesn't look so good . . . maybe another time . . . maybe never . . .
Friend 5 (*now alone*): Four days? How about three? I can do it in three days . . .

Yes, alas, you've played the part of hapless Friend 5 for far too long. It is with you in mind that we offer this simple guide to clip and save. Take out your weekend bag, open your closet and dresser drawers, and make at least one practice run with our "Guide to Practical Packing":

1) **Croquet mallets and wickets:** You want to stay in shape while you're away from home, yet you can't very well pack your hang glider, now can you? A hopeless dilemma? Perhaps, until you remember that most croquet sets come complete with a streamlined wooden case that fits snugly in any weekend bag. (To save room, scrape

off excess dirt and dried grass from wickets. There'll be plenty of mud—in the country!)

2) **Wet bar:** After a pickup game of croquet, what better way to relax than with a cool Bloody Mary or martini? Your wet bar away from home needn't weigh you down any more than absolutely necessary. Follow the simple *Esquire* checklist:

- 4 brandy snifters
- 2 highball glasses
- 1 bottle gin
- 1 bottle vodka
- a wisp of vermouth
- Snappy-Tom tomato juice
- 1 stalk celery
- 1 olive
- another olive
- 12 ice cubes

3) **Smoking Jacket:** (silk outer shell; cotton inner lining; two packs of cigarettes.) Just because you're relaxing around the base camp doesn't mean you should relax your sartorial standards. Remember: the better you look in your clothes, the better they look on you!

4) **No-smoking jacket:** (silk outer shell; cotton inner lining; no cigarettes.) Just in case you're weekending it with someone who says, when offered a cigarette, "No thank you. I don't smoke"—an early indication that he or she indeed does not smoke.

5) **Cordless telephone:** Conversations in the country can be intoxicating: "Look at that lovely bird." "Yes, it is a lovely thing." "So light and free. And lovely." "And *there's* a lovely cloud." Intoxicating, yes. But there's no need to get fall down *drunk* on these conversations. Call your office, your home and other friends, and force yourself to stay slightly sober, or you'll never be able to leave the country.

6) **Portable video camera and blank cassettes:** "Watch out for the cow dung!" "Who bent the wicket?" Fabulous moments—and you missed them because you were on the telephone. Let your friends capture these special times on tape so that you can relive them in the comfort and privacy of your den upon your return home.

7a) **Belts:**
- green canvas belt with brass buckle for days
- tan leather belt with silver buckle for early evenings
- black lizard belt with mother-of-pearl buckle for late evenings or

7b) **Suspenders:**
- green canvas suspenders for days
- tan leather suspenders for early evenings
- black lizard suspenders for late nights

8) **Framed portrait of Mother:** No man is at his best if he's forgotten his mother. The man of the eighties is confident enough to remind his friends that, "Hey, I've got a mother, and I'm just a little bit proud of her."

OPTIONAL ACCESSORIES

1) **Underwear:** Space permitting, a change of underwear (boxer shorts or BVDs) can make the weekend all the more pleasant for you and for your companion. We suggest that you follow the *Esquire* Undergarment Grid:

Number of Days Away from Home	Number of Underwear
1	1
2	2
3	3

The *Esquire* grid is based on a mathematical equation: n days away = n pairs of underwear, or $(n + 1)$ days away = $(n + 1)$ pairs of underwear.

Friend 1: Ready to go?!

Friend 5: Yes, this time.

Friend 2: Hey, Friend 5, like those snazzy black lizard suspenders!

Friend 5: Thanks.

Friend 3: Oh no! We forgot the croquet wickets.

Friend 5: No, we—

Friend 1: Aw, croquet's for sissies!

Friends 2, 3, 4: Right you are . . . uh-huh . . . yup . . . ol' sissy game, that's all . . .

Friend 5 (*to himself*): Darn, could've used that space for underwear.

Friend 1: What's that smell? That smells like 2.

Pyramid Comix

by Conan C. O'Brien (1985)

Have I Just Had Sex?
An Easy Self-help Test

by Christopher L. Dingman (1985)

Too often, it seems, after a night out with that girl you've had your eye on, your roommate will pose that thorny question, "Well, did you get laid?" In response to which you turn over hundreds of different pieces of evidence and thousands of possible ways to answer him while concealing your confusion. Finally, wishing to look cool but unwilling to state what might be completely wrong, you mumble, "Pretty much," and flop on the bed as if entirely worn out.

"Did I?" you think. You'd love to believe it, but who are you to say? "Have I just had sex . . . or not?"

So have you been out "stripping the paint with one of those heat guns" or is it just a false alarm? We hope the answer is you know what, and we don't mean the second one mentioned, the one about the false alarm.

Here's our easy six-step guide. Your friends will be astounded as you confidently reel off a response to your roommate's query. Good luck!

Illustrations by
Lawrence M.
Guterman

1) The first thing to remember is that there are only *two* answers to this question. They are "yes" and "no." Many people become confused (especially if more than one person is waiting to hear the answer) and frantically begin to think there exists a whole range of responses. "Pretty much," "mildly," "70 percent sure," "in many cultures what I did would be considered sex," and "I'm cautiously optimistic," however, are not acceptable answers.

2) If in grave doubt whether or not you've had sex that night, chances are you didn't. Remember, there will be a majority of occasions on which you'll not have had sex. This is why "the act" has at one time or another been labeled "the elusive thing," "the sweet thing," and "copulation."

3) Check yourself with this simple test: hold your right hand out flat in front of you with your palm down. If your hand is very jittery you will never make a good surgeon.

4) Ask your roommate the same question! "I don't know, smarty-pants, did you?" This will buy you valuable time, during which you can search for more clues. If this proves futile, ask him what he thinks. He probably knows you pretty well and will often be able to make a decision that is every bit as informed as your own. If the two of you disagree, you can always do rock-paper-scissors to see who is right.

5) Try this simple exercise: Think of the last time you could have sworn you had sex, and see how clearly tonight's experience matches up with it. Don't be misled by mere coincidences, however. The fact that you had chicken for dinner both nights is not indicative of similar *sexual* experiences.

6) If you still can't tell, give your date a ring and ask her to verify your final verdict. If you find out that you did have sex, make sure that she did too. Otherwise, something's getting lost in the shuffle. Far from being a cop-out, this technique ensures ultimate certainty. Your date, too, will appreciate your sensitivity.

A Plea for Subscribers
in the Form of a Dior Ad

(1985)

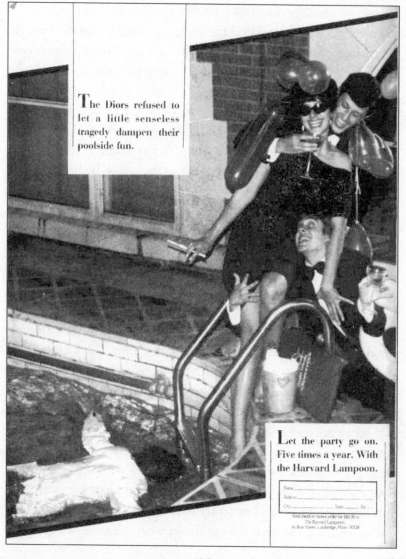

The Gambler

by Ted L. Greenberg (1985)

A hustler, a self-saboteur, a brinksman: you've seen him. He's on every street corner in America inching off the curb in anticipation of the light, but you probably know him as smiling Al the town barber or grumpy Phil the pirate. In many ways, though, he is just like you or me. In point of fact, he is me. That's right, sometimes barber, moonlight buccaneer, habitual gambler, and voracious pedestrian—me.

I'll bet on anything: the horses, the dogs, the llamas, endangered species. What do I care? I don't have to clean up after them. You see, I am a gambler. I gamble. Often. You ever see *Guys and Dolls*? Roguish bunch of guys, right? I know all the songs. By heart. By the way, the name's Robert; it was slapped on me by my mother when I was born, and I guess the tag stuck ever since. No, better not tell me your name, I'll only betray you. As a matter of fact, I lost my mother ten years ago. I was extremely low on cash, so I had to stake her in a poker game. It proved to be the most exciting hand of the night, although you can well imagine after reading my opponent's superior cards, I wept. Like a little baby I wept. Sure, I can look back on it and laugh, but at the time, I wept. After all, that was no stranger I had squandered. But the experience sobered me and taught me an invaluable lesson: you really can't put a price on human life. Funny thing . . . gambling. Oh yeah. Mom fell off the card table after slipping on some chips and cracked her spine. It was a doleful day. Mom had been a big boost to me and a reliable backer. That's when the wife and I took up tennis. It didn't work, though; Barbara kept knocking the balls over the fence. Funny wife . . . Barbara. Now we have our own family, but unfortunately the old tendencies still persist. Recently, I gambled away my father's newlywed, and the other day when the baby needed new shoes, what does the ace gambler do? He blows a hundred bucks in a crap game, that's what. I could have bought young Snake Eyes an entire bin of shoes with that money.

I've finally come to realize (the hard way) that gambling's a disease and that I've got it. Luckily, there are cures for such diseases. In fact, I've just returned from my first treatment of electroconvulsive therapy, and boy, did it hit the spot. No kidding. I'm going back for two more sessions tomorrow. As you can tell, I'm well on my way to a speedy recovery; so next time you see me in your town, how about commissioning me for a haircut or some booty, and maybe I wouldn't constitute just another entire statistic.

Six Universal Questions That Your Mother Never Told You About

by Elizabeth M. Losh (1985)

1. Whatever becomes of today's letter after *Sesame Street* is done with it?

The letter **G** runs a white slavery ring in the Bahamas. The letter **Q** is serving a ten-year sentence for relations with an unconsenting lowercase letter. The letter **S** now operates a lithium treatment center and halfway house for ex–Junior League Presidents in the Berkshires. He spends his weekends deprogramming cheerleaders. The letter **L** apologized to the American public for the words: lox, lascivious, and llama. The letter **B** founded a religious cult where worshippers spell themselves into a religious ecstacy and then beat each other brutally with pita bread.

2. Who was I in a previous life?

You were a Latvian newt trader named Chad—after the country where lots and lots of people starve to death. You had an unhappy childhood and your father threw large, heavy objects at you whenever you misbehaved. Once, when you neglected to do the dishes, he threw the Aswan Dam, a six-pack of Diet Pepsi, and the Iwo Jima memorial at you. Luckily, he missed. Your mother slicked down her hair with lighter fluid. You feared for her life in hot weather. Your sister caught lesbianism from a public toilet seat. Your dog overdosed on sleeping pills.

3. Why do socks disappear in the dryer?

Dryers are actually openings to alternate universes. In the past year alone, four Maytag repairmen were sucked into the dimension where people go through the larval stage. A Brunswick apartment dweller reached in to retrieve the fabric softener sheet and plunged headfirst into a universe populated by Dr. Seuss characters. She was carried off by an insane mob of blue fuzzy creatures shouting "Boil that dustspeck, boil that dustspeck!" Socks pass through onto a planet where they are the dominant life-form and where they grow and multiply, using peanut butter as slave labor. Their language is based on different inflections of the word "pulchritude," and they compose epic poems in it, based on the yearly harvest of waxy yellow buildup. They are a peaceful race.

4. How do I make a million dollars?

Sell your life story to *Soldier of Fortune* magazine. Invent a cuddly stuffed animal with nuclear capability. Tell people you want to have Gore Vidal's baby. Raise your children in Radio Shack and then go on lots of talk shows and tell people about it. Convince your parents to pay your tuition in unmarked bills with nonconsecutive serial numbers by a Dumpster in a dark alley. Collect cans. Open a lemonade stand. Start a lint farm and make your own clothing. Create a charge card for cigarette machines.

5. What is the key to a happy and successful life?

Cake decorations that look like steel pellets.

6. What will the future hold?

There will be a television miniseries called *Rich Man, Blind Man.* People will decorate their Christmas trees with diet pineapple chunks. The Partridge Family will stage a junta and rule the country. Big Bird will become the national symbol. The radio will become obsolete; people will play music only on Touch-Tone phones.

Burger Shed

by Paul R. Simms (1985)

I worked at Burger Shed this summer, and had some laughs. It was pretty much fun. I mean, this guy Ned who worked there, he really cuts up good sometimes, but the boss doesn't mind. Larry, the manager, says that joking around is good for morale and productivity as long as you maintain a clean Christian attitude about it. Larry always cuts out cartoons and tapes them to the door of his office. But the cartoons are always pictures of two guys sitting on an island fishing, saying, "When are we going to catch some of those REALLY BIG FISH?!" Larry gets a kick out of this.

Anyway, this is how the whole thing started. We got this immigrant guy who works out there—a thick-looking guy who speaks English well enough to be understood, but not well enough to be taken seriously. I don't think he goes to school or anything, and he's worked there longer than anyone else. This is the thing: the guy looks so much like a monkey that it's incredible. Just like a monkey. So every single day, at least once or twice, Ned says, "Hey, everybody! We got a monkey flipping burgers on grill number three!" And everyone laughs, and the immigrant guy just grins and keeps flipping burgers. I guess he thinks that "monkey" is just a name American guys call each other—like "badass" or "dude."

No one really thought much about this, but Ned said it at least once every single day. Anyway, one afternoon, the immigrant guy walks into work wearing this really heavy wool overcoat and grinning from ear to ear like a big happy monkey. He's flipping burgers and just sweating like you wouldn't believe, but he won't take the coat off. I figured it was some Old World tradition or something.

After a while, Ned looks up from the french fry machine and yells, "Hey, everybody! Look out! We got a sweaty monkey on grill number three!"

Suddenly, the guy pulls open his overcoat and out jumps one of those monkeys that has a little tiny body and a great big head. And the guy says, "Yes indeed, now we are certainly having a monkey on grill number three! Yes indeed, we are now having a *real* monkey on grill number three!"

It was hilarious, and everyone was just cracking up. Apparently the guy's uncle is an organ grinder at the carnival. Even Ned pointed his finger at the guy in a gun shape, and clicked his tongue and winked and said, "Got me . . ." One of the counter girls wanted to pet the monkey, but when she got close, the thing just started shrieking and mewling. It jumped off the guy's shoulder onto the hot grill. So this monkey is hopping up and down in a big cloud of smoke like a furry jumping bean, but even noisier. Finally, it hops off the grill and crawls into the broken opening to the AC vent. Everyone was pretty wigged out, and one of the counter girls was crying because she thought we'd killed it. Then to top it all off, Larry walks in. He looks at all of us, then looks up at the ceiling and exhales.

It was at that moment that we all noticed the smell. That little monkey's feet must sure be burned up some, I thought. We all kind of looked at the ground real quiet. Finally, Ned saves the day.

"Larry," he says, "I think we got a bad batch of meat here."

Larry sniffs one of the raw patties and says, "Yeah. Better throw it out."

Then Ned says, "Someone at the plant must have been monkeying around on the job." We all set to laughing and almost split a gut. Larry just kind of looked around and grinned 'cause he wasn't in on it.

"Yes, Ned," he said. "Someone must have."

That's probably the funniest thing that happened there. But there's other stuff too. Sometimes Ned would put two heads of lettuce down his apron and say, "Look, I'm a girl." We all laughed, because he wasn't. And this British guy worked there for a while, and he told all of us what "wank" means. So instead of saying "Thank you—come again" to customers, we started saying "Wank you—come again." No one else noticed it, but we got a kick out of it. Then one day some of the guys from the college rugby teams came in to eat, and one of the counter girls said, "Wank you very much," and the guy just reached across and tagged her a good one in the face. Maybe this just shows how some people can't take a joke. But no one said it much after that.

So it was a good summer. The funny thing is, no one ever found the monkey. They fixed the AC vent the next day. I think he got trapped in there and died, but his corpse hasn't gone bad because he died right over the walk-in freezer, where it's real cold. Someone else said that the vent opens outside, so he must have gotten away. But Ned says that the monkey is still up in the vent, growing to full gorilla size so that some day he can bust out and take his position at grill number three.

Nader's Raiders of the Lost Ark

by Conan C. O'Brien (1985)

The Kellogg Archipelago

by Greg M. Daniels (1985)

Illustration by Sarah J. Albee

Even the rats have ears in the Kellogg. I tell the rats nothing of importance, only what I want them to hear. But in the Soviet Union, rats are not companions, they are one of the four food groups. The only rats we have left in Kellogg 15 are the females. We are trying to milk them. Yuri, who has been without a woman the longest of us—but I digress.

Would you like to know a funny Russian joke I heard yesterday in the gruel line? Misha: In what country does the Secret Police beat the peasants, rape their women, and steal their food? Grisha: Not in Russia! In Russia, the peasants have no food! Ha-ha, I laugh until I cough out a tooth. Do you believe me? You are a fool. I have no teeth.

It is good that the Russian peasant can maintain his sense of humor.

I will tell you the stories of my fellow prisoners. Though they take our teeth, they cannot keep us silent!

Mikhail Urinski was given twenty years for peeing in the snow next to his apartment building in Minsk. Snow is another of the Soviet Union's four food groups.

"Fatty" Spratsonov was given thirty years because he did not laugh when a party chairman told that joke I heard in the gruel line.

Vladimir Gregorievitch Tadascibeuski was sent to the Kellogg when he was five days old because his name was too long.

184

Cyril Romanov was given ten years because he resembled Anton Gavrilovitch. Anton Gavrilovitch received sixty-five years after Cyril Romanov sent a baked ham to the judge.

Katya Ovanova got sixty years with hard labor really because she is so ugly.

Alexei Popov got a year for wearing stupid clothes;

Arkady Momov still is here for singing through his nose;

Fyodor Pavelovitch got twenty years for the love of a chairman's daughter;

Yuri Mikhailovitch got twenty years for drinking too much water;

And Vlad Yuriolov is a little piggy and got seven years with hard labor.

Did you like those last five? That is our camp song. And there are more.

Gabor Dyslexovitch got twelve years for reading backward.

Vidal Oscalov is here because he makes puns. They will never let him leave. Actually, I don't blame them; he makes terrible puns.

Nicholas Golobov got twenty years because he looks Japanese, but isn't, and it's just too confusing and boring to listen to him explain all about it.

Johan Finkelovitch too is a bore, and that is why he is here. The system does have some merits.

And finally, Yoyo Yablonski received twelve years for stealing coal. Coal is the third major food group in the Soviet Union.

These, then, are the histories of my bunkmates. Why am I here? I am here because suffering begets consciousness, and I must be conscious to write of the soul of Mother Russia, which is made of suffering, and of her body, which is the people. Also, I held up a package store in the Nevsky Prospect. I am afraid, however, that my words, my testament, will never reach the West. This is not because I fear that the Secret Police, those bumbling oppressors, will confiscate my papers; a canny Russian with the indomitable will that only the furnace of suffering can forge may often outwit the police. Rather, it is because paper is the fourth major food group of the Soviet Union, and all I had for lunch today was snow.

Advice Column:
Your Penny's Worth

by Richard J. Appel and Jonathan A. Shayne (1985)

YOUR PENNY'S WORTH

In last week's column, we were discussing how to save money in your personal life—you know, with pocketbooks, pencils, desks, calendars, watches, paper, the kids' education, your health, and magazine subscriptions. You can save even more money in your personal life with these pointers.

Beauty Aids: How many ways can you think of to use lipstick? That's right, there's only one. But a ChapStick and red food coloring can do the job nicely—and there is so much more that a Chap-Stick can do: the kids can use it as a paste stick in their arts and crafts class, you can use it to "ChapStick" the cookie sheet instead of using butter, and Dad can use it on his hair to recapture the look of the Roaring Twenties. And if you have a complete set of food colorings, then you've also bought your last eye shadow.

In Your Car: What do you do on those cold winter mornings when your hand touches that frigid ring of plastic known as the steering wheel? You probably just grin and bear it. But you don't have to. Take some bubblepack—that plastic bubble paper used in packing—and wrap it around your wheel. A touch of paste on the inside lip of the bubble strips should hold it nicely (if you haven't already switched to ChapStick). If you have any bubblepack left over, then you've got yourself the perfect stocking stuffer for next Christmas.

"Kids! It's dinnertime. Wash your hands!" That's a familiar mealtime call. But next time you sing that melody, add this chorus, "Don't use any of our water!"

The routine need be altered only slightly: take the bar of soap in hand, rub both sides and up by the wrists too. Of course, without water, one needs to scrub with a little more diligence.

Christmas Cards: Because I am a well-known and respected syndicated columnist, I receive hundreds of Christmas cards each December. It used to break my heart to throw them out. But from now on, Christmas will be truly joyous because I've discovered a way to reuse them.

Many of the cards I get are lushly illustrated and engraved. Let's take an example: I get a card with a snowman on the front, and on the inside, engraved in red, is the message: "Season's Greetings from the Huntingtons." To that I add, in my own hand, "and from Marv and Penny Stumplemeyer." It looks pretty good. Next year I send the card to one of my friends.

One reminder: The Gilmores or the Krauts might be more interested in receiving the card than the Huntingtons themselves.

Your Kids: People often write to me about one of the most difficult situations: a young child with an obsessive desire for an expensive luxury. For instance, I've heard of many girls who want ponies. In my own family, Billy insisted on being given a polyphonic synthesizer and wouldn't settle for anything less.

I gave him a checkers set.

And suppose you want to be a successful syndicated columnist, like me. Don't rush out and buy a $250 typewriter or, for heaven's sake, one of those $2,000 word processors. "Then how will I write?" you ask. The answer is simple and inexpensive.

You probably remember when your children were little that you punched out name labels for them on adhesive plastic strips with a rotary letter punch. You know, if your child's name was Sam, you'd rotate the dial to *S*, punch, then rotate the dial to *A*, and punch again, then *M*, and punch and scissor and you've got SAM. Then you'd remove the paper backing and stick the label on his notebook. Well, if you're like me, you have yards and yards of unused green plastic label tape and a rotary letter puncher that's just gathering dust! Here's the key to your future success as a syndicated columnist, like me. Punch, peel, stick—punch, peel, stick—and you'll be on your way to a lucrative career as a print journalist, without having to buy an expensive typewriter, which, after all, is only good for typing.

If the adhesive on your label tape has worn out, no problem: just use some ChapStick.

If you follow my simple advice, you'll be pinching so many pennies that you'll have to pinch yourself too—to realize that you're not dreaming.

Sex

by Glenn P. McDonald (1986)

*S*ex, I thought as I turned the corner.

   Figs, I thought as I passed a big sign that said, "Figs."

Sex, I thought again. I don't like figs.

I was on my way to a rendezvous with Destiny. An encounter with Fate. A *Geschaltergammenwienerlung*.

I was going to buy a book. It's a special book, a book called *173 Tips for People Who Are Obsessed with Sex but Really Still Think "Orgasm" Is the Sound of a Golden Retriever Throwing Up.*

Okay, fine, laugh. Yeah, go on. You who are so sophisticated in the world, you who can chuckle knowingly at tall buildings and trains and all . . . I just had different priorities stressed in my upbringing than you did. Like cold oatmeal. And hooded robes, and chants, and walking around with my hands clasped together.

Gosh. Mom was a nutty one.

To tell the truth, I didn't find out what sex was until someone corrected me for using *contraception* as a synonym for good dental hygiene my senior year in high school.

But, man, did I learn quick. Within three months I could point out the genitals on a moving woman from twenty feet away. By the time I left for college, I'd decided that sex was going to be as much a part of my life as, oh, figs. Well, nearly, anyway.

Somehow things didn't work out. I'd introduce myself to a girl, and then she'd run away, and then . . . That next step always eluded me. The transition from her one moment flagging down motorcycle gangs or seven-year-olds on bicycles in her haste to escape, to the next moment the two of us being together in the nonclothed sense of the term just never panned out for me.

I tried lines. I tried lines: "Dahling. I think you and me could make beautiful mucus together." "If I told you I'd respect you in the morning, would you hold it against me?" "Hey, baby, wanna see my edging?" Nothing seemed to work. Something about me just turned them off.

I graduated from college still a virgin who hadn't had sex. The closest I'd come to intercourse was when I accidentally hit my ball from the pink section to the blue section playing miniature golf. No matter, I figured. Now that I'm out in the world, offers will pile up on my doorstep like dead birds.

Well, once again, things didn't turn out quite like I'd hoped. When the third girl at Madame Erotica's House of Phone Sex told me she had a headache, I decided it was time to do some serious research. About then I started shuffling through my back issues of the newsletter of the Cold Shower of the Month Club in which I found the advertisement for the book in question.

As I walked to the bookshop I leered wistfully at the women crossing the street and casually crawling down rusty storm drains to avoid me. Soon they would all be mine, right there in the street.

Well, maybe not in the street. But lots and lots of sex, that's the key part.

I hummed a little farewell to whatever bizarre character flaw of mine so revolted all things feminine, and then I reached the store.

As I went through the low doorway, I stooped carefully to avoid hurting the mallard that always sits on my head squawking "Fuck! Fuck! Fuck!" Pretty soon, I thought, this duck and I are going to see some *real* action.

Catalog Ads

by Paul R. Simms (1986)

Smoke Detector: Will detect smoke in your kitchen, living room, attic, or any other area within a fifty-mile radius. Never stops buzzing. Batteries extra. ($3.00)

Retarded Cats: Biometrics lab going out of business, didn't have the heart to kill these poor mentally retarded cats. Remarkably ugly; will eat anything. ($3.00)

Backyard Gnome with Exposed Penis: The gnome needs a home. Lovingly hand-carved by former employee. ($3.00)

Swiss Watch: This wristwatch is so finely tuned and copiously oiled that it can do in one hour what it takes other watches days to do. ($3.00)

30-Foot Ladder on Wheels: Slightly harder to use, but easier to move around. Fun for some. ($3.00)

Mirrored Shades: These "cool-guy" shades are mirrored on the inside. Perfect for sitting around and staring into your own eyes. Not for the emotionally unstable. ($3.00)

Brooklyn Bridge: Official Certificate of Ownership entitles you to own large bridge in New York City. Please enclose money order, delivery address, immigration papers. ($3.00)

Rodin's "Thinker" Statue with Exposed Penis: You can probably guess what's on his mind. Perfect novelty gift, party favor, weighs one ton. ($3.00)

Miniature Cuisinart: So small that the first thing it slices and dices is itself. Watch it go. ($3.00)

Miscolored Blacklight Poster: Sexy naked woman with glowing green pubic beard. ($3.00)

"Accolades": Receive gushing kudos from Rex Reed, Jeffrey Lyons on your own film, novel, or family Christmas newsletter. Available to you at the same prices the major studios pay. ($3.00)

Spat Rack: Hang up your spats on this delightful rack. ($3.00)

Big Dead Fish with Used Cigar in Its Mouth: Unpleasant but priced to move. ($3.00)

Gardening Equipment: Rake, hedge trimmer, weed wacker. We borrowed them from the people next door, never returned them. ($3.00)

Penis Extending Device: Actually extends length of the male member. Stretches penis to minimum of two feet or snapping point, whichever comes first. ($3.00)

Automated Bullet Dispenser: Cash-operated vending machine ejects bullets at potentially injurious velocity. South American dictatorship reneged on their original order. Could be a money-maker in some areas. ($3.00)

Red Velour Pants: Looks good, feels good. Perfect gift for grandchildren. Also good for monkeys and other animals who can be made to wear clothes. ($3.00)

Life-at-a-Glance Daily Planner: Keep track of important appointments, from youth to middle age to predeath. Good through year 2065; includes zip codes for entire continental U.S. and future colonies on Omicron 5 and the ghost planet Rigel 7.

Annual Sale of Slightly Damaged and Irregular Merchandise

Grab Bag: Mystery sack contains no more than 5 "jive-turkey" style personal items. Not for the easily surprised. ($3.00)

Clown Bus: Brightly colored Volkswagen Microbus seats 5,000. Clown around and go in style. That's an order. ($3.00)

Reversible Corduroy Body Buddy: Luxuriate in the plush microtroughs of this miracle fabric. Hear it whisper sweet nothings to the secret places of your bare body. Available in beige and brown. ($3.00)

Frenchman's Wife: Naughty Frenchman is off making hanky-panky with some other woman; left his wife unattended. She wants nothing more than to please you and to avoid bathing. ($3.00)

Dog Phone: Longer range than standard dog whistles. Encodes all sound into inaudible hyperfrequencies to fool human eavesdroppers. ($3.00)

Smoking Monkey: Eliminate the bad-time blues and surplus tobacco simultaneously with this actual smoking orangutan. ($3.00)

Sour Mash Mouth Melts: Fermented corn bootleg moonshine top-skim compressed into edible pellets. ($3.00)

Organically Grown Human Head: It frowns, it winks; it talks, it thinks. When you weary of conversation, simply submerge it in its tank. Hair food extra. ($3.00)

Board Stretcher: First day on the job? You'll need one of these. Special bonus offers also receive left-handed screwpusher full of sky-hooks (variety of sizes and velocities). ($3.00)

Drinking Dog: Plush toy mock-up of generic beer company's famous mascot. Added bonus: Famous Name Person pliable figurine. ($3.00)

Satin Tour Jacket: Look like a record company asshole for less than half the price. ($3.00)

Wolf Whistle: Mouth-size metal implement allows you to cut loose with the famous "wolf whistle." Sure to be a big hit with the kind of women who go for construction workers and garbagemen. ($3.00)

Elvis Auto: The only set of wheels classy enough to bear Elvis's personal name. Altered '73 Townhawk is shaped just like Elvis on all fours; wheels at hands and knees. You sit in Elvis's mouth and drive around. ($3.00)

Little White Lies

by Maya C. M. Forbes (1990)

Tim Noyes says yes to a second helping of his grandmother's eggplant casserole; the rest of the family is instantly full. When Grandma bends over to dish it out, they grin and pretend like they're throwing up under the table. It takes him hours to finish, and eventually he is alone at the table. He tries to slip it to the dog. He tries to roll it up in a napkin. He tries to eat it. His grandmother comes in periodically but never once offers to take it away.

OUTCOME: **Tim hates his grandmother.**

Jerry Lyne feels obliged to say his best friend's two-hundred-pound "little" sister would be cute if she only lost some weight. So she fasts for a day, sits in a hot oven wrapped in Saran Wrap, drops eight pounds, and Jerry is forced to take her to the movies every night for a week. Lucky for him, she's very receptive to the HUGE Tub O'Corn with Extra Butter at the concession stand and she puts the weight back on in no time. Jerry is then able to tell his friend that the problem seems inconquerable, as does the sister.

OUTCOME: **Jerry hates his best friend.**

Wilma Norris is watching television over at the Lanes' house. It is turned up to a deafening level but no one else seems to notice. Mrs. Lane yells to Wilma, and Wilma says "What?!?" Mrs. Lane yells again and Wilma says "What?!?" Mrs. Lane yells again, Wilma gets up to go over to her, trips over the extension cord, falls down, breaks her nose in four places, and no one asks her to the senior prom.

OUTCOME: **Wilma hates extension cords and all that goes with them.**

Harold Thomas lets his son James beat him at everything from touch football to relay races. As a result, James grows up to be a big dumb asshole without any kind of support from anyone, anywhere.

OUTCOME: Harold hates his son.

Dan Burke is asked by a woman if he'll marry her daughter, and she phrases it in such a way that no matter what he says it doesn't really mean no. When he tries to officially propose to Samantha, she alternates between crying hysterically in the corner and touching his ear with her fingers. In the end they are wed.

OUTCOME: Dan hates his life.

A Call for Subscribers

(1990)

Politically Correct Jokes
for Your Knee-jerk Friends

by Dan J. O'Keefe (1991)

Having trouble remembering exactly what you're supposed to be feeling guilty about this week? Do your friends' jerking knees kick you in the balls for not owning the new Tracy Chapman album, and for owning Crosby Stills & Nash only on CD when vinyl is so much more *sincere*? Ever wish they'd all blown up on the Rainbow Warrior? Well, here's your chance: while they're out at the protest march, study these jokes and instantly become the biggest thing in PC circles since sliced whole-grain bread. Then again, they might misunderstand and beat you to death with their acoustic guitars. Those people are so *sensitive*, you know.

Q: Why did the chicken cross the road?
A: Because sexuality is a continuum!

Guy walks into a bar and bets the bartender he can piss clear across the bar without a drop hitting the ground and knock a mug of beer off the end of the counter. Barkeep says you're on, so the guy whips out his pecker and lets fly. Sure enough, the man's powerful stream blasts the mug into the jukebox without a drop touching the counter, and yet neither man could free himself from the phallo-centric discourse that envelops us all.

And then there's the one about the university professor whose tenure was revoked because he wasn't sensitive to the needs of women and minorities!

A Christian, a Muslim, and a Jew meet at the gates of heaven, and realize before long that all cultures are equally valid.

Knock, knock.
Who's there?
I cannot answer that question, as I have been robbed of my true identity by exploitative white-male-dominated society.

How many postmodern feminist theorists does it take to screw in a lightbulb?
Your question reveals that you subscribe to an antifeminist and antihuman world view in which it is assumed that said theorists can and will be forced to screw in said lightbulb by means of the implicit threat of violence against marginalized individuals that holds our corrupt society together.

Dear Julian

by Alec H. Berg (1991)

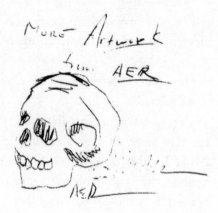

Dear Julian,

I'm having a dinner party this weekend, and I want to prepare a veal and chicken marsala. My question is, since veal is red meat and chicken is white meat, what type of wine should I serve?

L.R., Passaic, N.J.

Dear L.R.,

Couldn't you just serve one of those blush wines or something . . . I don't know . . . something.

Dear Julian,

Recently the trap under my sink rusted out, and I was forced to replace it. When the guy at the hardware store told me that it would cost a hundred and twenty-eight fifty to replace the thing, you can bet I told him where to stick it. I went right down to the auto-parts store, bought a couple of feet of radiator hose, and slapped that on the old sink. It works like a charm. Whaddya think?

B.F., Canton, Ohio

Dear B.F.,

It sounds good, I guess. If you're happy with it, then, you know, whatever . . . something . . . I don't know . . . I think I'm gonna puke.

Dear Julian,

My girlfriend and I have discovered something amazing. If I bathe in guacamole before we make love, I can sustain erection for up to fourteen hours. Do you have any explanation for this? Do you know of any other way of getting these results? Have you ever sported wood for fourteen hours?

A.E., Cambridge, Mass.

Dear A.E.,

I think if you put a little lime juice in guacamole, it won't turn brown . . . or maybe it's lemon juice . . . or something . . . I'm not sure.

Dear Julian,

Have you ever met Menudo?

P.P., Acres, Iowa

Dear P.P.,

I saw one of those guys on TV once, when I was sick . . . or just tired, I can't remember . . . forget it . . .

Dear Julian,

Is it me, or do you sound depressed? Perhaps you should take a little time off. Go to Europe, see the sights. Play outside, sing some songs, breathe the fresh country air. You know, live a little.

B.D., Portland, Ore.

Dear B.D.,

Did your folks do a lot of drugs or something? . . . No, that was a cheap shot . . . I'm sorry . . . whatever . . . Christ, look at me, I'm shaking like a fish.

Elvis Has Left the Building

by Robert M. Carlock (1992)

Announcer: Elvis has left the building!

Teenage Fans: (*Scream!*)

Announcer: Elvis has forgotten his coat and has now reentered the building!

Teenage Fans: (*Scream!*)

Announcer: Elvis has left the building, again.

Security: All right, everyone, clear out.

Announcer: Elvis has locked his keys in his car and has again reentered the building!

Teenage Fans: Really?

Security: Oh.

Announcer: Elvis is now inside the building, looking for a coat hanger!

Teenage Fans: Use my coat hanger, Elvis! Ooooh! No! Use mine! Here's a coat hanger, Elvis!

Announcer: Elvis has now left the building for a third time.

Teenage Fans: I didn't even get to see him. He took my coat hanger! Did you all see that? He's so dreamy!

Announcer: Elvis still can't open his car and has yet again reentered the building, now in tears!

Group of Bullies: Ha-ha! Elvis, what a baby! Why don't you get out of the building, Elvis? It's *our* building.

Announcer: Elvis has left the building!

Teenage Fans: What a pansy.

Vegas Weatherman

by David H. Mandel and John Aboud III (1992)

"Okay, you got the fountain in the background. Let's get this in one ... two ... three ... Hi there, Las Vegas. It's a beautiful day for—"

"Hey, buddy."

"Excuse me?"

"You're the weather guy, right?"

"Yeah ..."

"Gonna rain on Saturday, right?"

"Uh, no."

"I said, it's gonna rain Saturday."

"No. I checked the satellite an hour ago. It's going to be clear and breezy, highs in the mid-eighties. I'm issuing a pollen alert."

"I got a friend who would be very interested in seeing some rain on Saturday. I think it would be also in your best interest if it were to rain on Saturday."

"Yeah, and what if I don't?"

"You've been having some trouble with the humidity. My client could make that all disappear. Also, wind chill. And we wouldn't want anything going wrong with the barometric pressure."

"Are you threatening me?"

"I have not threatened you. I am a big fan of the weather. I admire your work very much."

"I know all the big weather guys. Who do you work for?"

"My client prefers anonymity."

Dear Big Moose

by Elijah Aron, Josh B. Lieb, and Lewis Morton (1992)

Dear Mister Moose,

I am like you, the Moose. I am not a brainy "intellectual" who savages innocent people with mysterious "brain powers" like the other characters in your comic books do. Does Jughead wear a crown because he is the king of Riverdale High? Perhaps you should give that Jughead the only kind of sandwich he can't eat—a knuckle sandwich! Yeah, the Moose! Hail, King Moose! Yeah!

Good-bye!

Tob Tobler

P.S. My name is supposed to be "Tom" but I have a cold.

Big Moose Responds:

Although I appreciate your support, I suppose I ought to let you know that I'm not actually as stupid as I appear to be in the comic periodicals. As an actor, I feign stupidity for the public's amusement; you'll notice that people laugh at *stupid you* all the time. Although I'm not a genius in the league of Forsythe P. "Jughead" Jones (a Phi Beta Kappa at Wisconsin U., if you can believe it!), I am a human being of average intelligence. Keep those letters coming!

Dear Moose,

Does anyone know where the stick I always hit myself in the head with is? Oh, there it is.

Never mind,

Lionel

Big Moose Responds:
   Keep those letters coming!

Dear Archie,
   Regarding your query of the seventeenth, viz who am I taking to the big dance this weekend: I think I'll take Big Moose's girl, Midge. I know Moose is fanatically jealous, but I am at this very moment sending him a letter that will convince him he needs to be in Central City that weekend for a football practice! I only hope I don't get these letters mixed up (ha-ha)!

                        Your sneaky friend,
                        Reggie

Big Moose Responds:
   Midge! Hey, that's my girl!

Dear Mister Big Moose,
   Are you in the comics portrayed in actual size? Because if you are, you're not so big and strong. You're tiny. I'm maybe a million times bigger than you. Do you want to fight? Look, I'm taking tiny Midge to be my pet! She loves kissing me because I'm B-I-G! This drives you crazy, doesn't it?
                        Signed,
                        Jake "Jokey" Jefferson

Big Moose Responds:
   I guess you caught me, Jake. I'm not really a very big guy at all. Similarly, I'm not really Midge's boyfriend. I just act like boyfriend and girlfriend. However, while I would not get insanely jealous because Midge is not my girlfriend, she is a good friend of mine because we work so closely—so I would prefer you did not bother her.

Dear Archie,

Regarding your query of the twentieth, viz why did I send you Big Moose's letter: I sent you Big Moose's letter?! Why, that means I must have sent Moose the letter I meant to send to . . . yipe!!!

Your Scared Friend,
Reggie!

Big Moose Responds:

I'm going to get that Reggie!

Dear Big Moose,

I would like to transfer to Riverdale High and hang out with Archie and the Gang. Maybe after high school, I could even go to State U. (not its archrival, Tech) with the rest of you fellas. Please tell me where is Riverdale.

Your soon to be buddy,
Leon Gross

Big Moose Responds:

I hate to break it to you, Leon, but Riverdale is not an actual school at all, but an elaborately constructed movie set. It might be easier for you to imagine Riverdale as a *state of mind.* In that way, we're all really going to Riverdale, aren't we? However, there are many good state universities in America, as well as many tech schools, which are also very fine. Keep those letters coming!

Dear Big Moose,

Um, you MUST go to practice in Central City this weekend. It is VERY important. Um, if you got a funny letter from Reggie, uh—never mind that! Don't get Reggie! This is an order from the coach—don't get Reggie!

Love,
Coach Kleats (not Reggie)

Big Moose Responds:

Oooh, I wish I could get that Reggie! It turns out he was right about that football practice, without even knowing it. The irony is delicious.

Well, I'm off to Central City! Keep those letters coming.

How Funny Is It?:
The Life of an MC

by J. Stewart Burns and Josh B. Lieb (1992)

ACT I

MC: Folks, welcome to the Mirage. I'm sorry, but there's no show tonight. The comedian is dead.

Man: More like drunk, eh?

MC: No, it's true. He died of a heart attack.

Lady: Give him an enema.

MC: Lady, he's dead! An enema can't help him now.

Lady: Can't hurt.

Man: Ha-ha-ha.

MC: Please, why don't you all just leave?

Lady: Not until we see him onstage.

MC: He can't get up! He's dead!

Man: I'll say he can't get it up.

Lady: He-he-he.

Man: Looks like she'd say that too.

MC: Please, folks, he's died backstage.

Lady: That's a change. Normally he dies onstage.

Man: Like you, MC.

MC: Lord, get me outta here!

ACT II

MC: Ladies and germs, welcome to the Flamingo!

Man: Did you just call me a germ?

MC: It's just a joke.

Man: Like if you said I was stupid, that would be a joke, right? If you called my wife ugly, that's a joke?

MC: Right.

Man: I want to see the manager.

MC: Please, sir, I was only kidding.

Man: But my wife is ugly.

MC: Lord, get me outta here!

ACT III

MC: Ladies and gentlemen, welcome to Caesar's! Please don't talk to me. I'm tired of being an MC.

Man: How tired are you?

MC: No, really, I'm so tired that . . .

Lady: That? That, what? What's the punch line?

MC: Please, ma'am, leave me alone. I just want to introduce our famous comedian.

Man: How famous is he?

MC: Not that famous, all right. You all are too much.

Lady: How much are we?

MC: If you all don't stop, I'll kill myself.

Man and lady: How much will you kill yourself?

MC: (*plunging knife into torso*) Lord, get me outta here.

ACT IV

God: Welcome to the heaven of dead comedians and MCs!

MC: Oh, how wonderful it is to be dead!

God: How wonderful is it?

MC: You're not in on this too, are you?

God: How in on it am I?

MC: Lord, get me outta . . . oh, damn.

God: Well?

MC: You're *so* in on it that . . .

Missy Manners

by Josh B. Lieb (1993)

Okay, so you're in the cafeteria. They're serving peas. The boy across from you is throwing peas like an expert into your milk carton. Proper etiquette response is, "Cool, man!"

A girl you do not like asks you to her dumb birthday party. What does etiquette say to do? Etiquette says, "Out-o-sight, man! I'll be there." Then don't go. If your mom finds out and makes you go, act weird at the party and make sure everyone can tell you've been crying. If the party is at Shakey's, don't eat any pizza, and don't eat cake no matter what! Or you'll have to be friends. Don't say thank you to the dumb mom.

Okay, enough free stuff. Here are your questions.

Dear Missy Manners:

My grandma gives me the wrong stuff, but I kiss her anyway. Then, later, my mom makes me write thank-you notes. Is this etiquette?

Gentle Reader:

First, when you get the wrong stuff, kiss Grandma but make sure she knows she screwed up. Say "Cool, Grandma . . . ," then go sit alone in your room and don't take the present with you. If your mom makes you write a note, etiquette says write it like, "Thank you for the present. I hate Mommy. I love you even though."

Dear Missy Manners:

My mom makes me have my birthday party with the red-headed boy because we have the same birthday. This is not fair!

211

Gentle Reader:

When the moms cut the cake and the boy's mom hands the first piece to you, don't eat it like it has cooties. Say, like etiquette, "Give it to Dee," and cry when they ask why. When Dee tries to get another piece say, "You have had enough." This is okay, because your mom knows you really hate this boy, but she is being cheap with the other mother, so she feels guilty. Don't say anything in the car home. Then say, "This is the worst birthday ever." This will make Mom cry.

A Cover from 1998

Cover by Justin A. Nowell

A Call for Subscribers

(1993)

Guinness Book of World Records

by Nicholas A. Stoller and Danny L. Tobey (1998)

THE WORLD'S LONGEST YARDSTICK
One yard long. (That's 36 inches!)

THE RECORD FOR LONGEST CONSECUTIVE BREATHING
Held by Doreen O'Callahan, who is coincidentally the world's longest living human. Known affectionally as "Old Lungs," Doreen has been breathing since 1897, when she turned twelve.

THE WORLD'S MOST CONTAGIOUS DISEASE
The Ebola virus. Kudos, Ebola virus!

THE WORLD'S TALLEST MIDGET
Brad Smith—measures nearly five feet nine inches tall. Despite being a midget, Brad lives a relatively normal life, except that he is constantly turned down for midget roles in movies for being "a poor actor."

THE FIRST PRESIDENT OF THE UNITED STATES
George Washington. Others would follow.

THE WORLD'S MOST RELIABLE CAR is the Honda Accord.

THE NICEST GUY IN THE WORLD
Todd. He's a real real real real real real real real real real real real real real real real real real real real real real real real real real real real real real real real real real real real real real real sweetheart. But we're just friends. I mean, come on. Since when was "nice" fun?

THE MAN WITH THE WORLD'S LONGEST FINGERNAILS
has cut his fingernails. He will not be featured in this year's book.

THE SHORTEST WORDS IN THE ENGLISH LANGUAGE
"I," "a," and "h." H is short for *herbiculture.*

**CLAUDE HOBSON, A LIBRARIAN, HAS READ THE
ENTIRE CORPUS OF WORLD LITERATURE**
More books than any other person! An illiterate by trade, Hobson
dabbles in reading and faking his way through high school by getting others to read for him. On his fortieth birthday, Hobson told
reporters, "What's that say?"

**THERE WILL BE NO OTHER MENTIONS IN THIS BOOK
OF THE MAN WITH THE WORLD'S LONGEST FINGER-
NAILS.**
We told him not to do it. He knew this would happen. He was
warned.

THE MOST INDIAN MAN
Mahatma Gandhi. He was born there, died there, and spent the
better part of his life there.

**JEFF, WHAT WERE YOU THINKING? THE NAILS,
MAN . . . YOU WERE FAMOUS.**

THE WORLD'S LONGEST LIMOUSINE is fifty-seven feet
long. It features a chandelier, bar, hot tub . . . oh, who are we kidding? We're hurtin' Jeff. And we're sorry. Come back. Shh. No more
talk. Just . . . come back.

I LOVE YOU.
The editors of the *Guiness Book of World Records* love each and every
one of you. You're all records in our book.

Grown-ups Remember . . . Monsters in the Bedroom

by Daniel Chun (1999)

For as much of my youth as I can remember, I was afraid of monsters. Every night I stared at the closet, afraid of what would come out. I was convinced that monsters lived there. I think it was because of the way my dad would whisper "Good night, monsters" every time he walked by my closet after tucking me in. He didn't think I heard him, but I did.

* * *

I had one monster who relentlessly haunted me for years. He called himself Caleb. Even when we moved to a different house, Caleb followed. He would come into my room and gargle his name late at night. Other nights I would wake up to his bloodcurdling shrieks. Why my parents never told me that I had a little brother is beyond me.

* * *

My older brother loved to scare me. One of his tricks was to hide under my bed at night. Then, when my parents left the room, he would reach up and grab me. The slick, scaly chill of his freak reptilian hand sure gave me fright.

* * *

I remember seeing the movie *Leprechaun* when I was little. For months afterward I was convinced that the villain from the movie was shuffling into my room late at night and staring at me. He would stand on his tiptoes to see over the edge of the bed, and then he would just stay there for hours, laughing every once in a while in his insane way.

I never figured out if it was my imagination or old Mr. Connelly, the senile Irish midget who rented out our basement apartment.

* * *

My parents were quite the pranksters, and they loved the way they could freak me out because of my irrational fear of monsters. I'll never forget the time they put on Halloween masks and popped out of my closet. So funny! I will also always remember the time they made a tape of scary sounds and stuck the tape player under my bed. We chuckled all week after that one. Similarly, my brain will always possess the hilarious memory of the time they built a trapdoor in my floor and decorated the cellar to resemble the bowels of hell. When I fell through the floor, they were there, dressed up as two cacodaemons, and they told me I was dead and condemned. I saw through their little ruse a few days later when Mom's costume tail fell off. I have such jovial parents.

* * *

My tainted childhood was one of wicked, violent thoughts occupying every pained second of my days and dreams. My mind was a grotesque canvas where the most sinister forms and silhouettes spun their evil danse macabre in a never-ending cycle of terror. Images of gothic horror poisoned my mind until I was forced to enter a mental institution. I think it was because of those Goosebumps book by R. L. Stine. Creepy to the max!

My Unhappy Rendezvous
with Magical Realism

by B. J. Novak (1999)

My travel agent suggested that I spend my paid vacation this year in a small coastal town in South America. It was the worst vacation ever. A lot of things went wrong.

Juanita was our chef for lunch the first day. She had just bid farewell to her lover, posted by the military to a distant port town. Her infinite tears spilled into the flour like raindrops while she cooked, expressing in taste what she was forbidden to tell with words. When she served the meal, each bite echoed with the unbearable sadness of Juanita's limitless heartbreak.

It was the worst burrito I ever had.

The next night I went to the town's annual talent show.

The first act was a young boy who sang with such beauty that the birds dropped dead from the sky of jealousy (but no one translated the song for me). Then came a melodramatic lady who, with great tears and fanfare, vanished permanently from the earth.

Finally after what seemed like forever, it was time for my magic trick.

"Ladies and hombres, I need an assistant. How about . . . you! Come on up!"

With a little luck and a lot of distraction techniques, I was able to bring the card the poor orphan girl was thinking about right to the front of the deck.

I heard a lot of nervous shuffling, but no applause.

"That is not a trick to us," one man finally offered. "That is the way the cards here always are."

Say what?

I quickly switched categories and tried to win for Most Ironic—

but that award went to some blind prophet who could tell how many fingers a person was about to hold up but never how many he was holding at the time.

At the awards ceremony, first prize turned out to be the undying love of a woman whose excess of sensual passion could melt all the snow of the Andes. I wondered aloud if she also had enough excess of detergent to get me clean towels. "Oh, that was the prize for Most Ironic," she smirked, with such excess of sarcastic force that the Amazon started to flow backward, flooding my hotel room and ruining a lot of my stuff.

The following evening I noticed an attractive lady sitting by herself at the town dance.

"What's your name?" I asked.

"I have no name," she whispered through closed lips.

"Beauty is nameless," echoed the wind.

"Can I get you a drink?"

With that she floated away, off the earth forever. She was too beautiful for the earth.

"Too pretty," sighed the man to my right.

"Yes, pretty," I repeated. (Pretty lame.)

Could anything save my trip? I thought at least I could get some good surfing in the next morning. I hiked down to the beach—but the damn ocean was as still as ice!

"In our town," explained the sage José Revuelto de Cementario, before turning into a spider, "those who stare at the moon by night erase its morning power over the waves." Or something like that—I wasn't really listening. "Perhaps you may surf on the sand."

Of course, José. That's *exactly* how surfing works.

It was time to put an end to this dumb vacation. In the town plaza, I found an old bookshop that I figured might sell a guidebook that could help me find a way to leave town.

This doorknob is loose, I thought as I entered.

"So, I hear, is the woman who bore thee," punned the mind-reading gypsy behind the counter, in English, absolutely embarrassing me as he handed me the guidebook. The store erupted in cold flames as I left, and frankly, I was glad.

It turned out the guidebook that the old gypsy had sold to me was not an ordinary guidebook, but an account of my own journey to the town. I skipped ahead a couple pages, and before long found the text predicting my reading of each word of the book as I read it. As I stared into my unfolding fate, present and future became one, my life and my destiny trapped together for eternity in an inescapable and endless hall of mirrors.

It was the most boring infinite stretch of time ever.

True Fairy Tale Classics

by Nicholas A. Stoller (1999)

The editors at *True Fairy Tale Classics* personally guarantee the realism you expect from a fairy tale. Read the following excerpts:

Rapunzel awoke from her slumber and approached the window. The prince cried up to her, "Rapunzel, let down your hair!" She cast down her golden locks in one big dread, unwashed as was the custom of her time. Free, finally free, to live with the prince in eternal bliss! Like 36 percent of Merovingian females, Rapunzel would be dead of dysentery by age twenty-eight.

"The Flying Carpet works on simple aerodynamic principles," exclaimed the anxious genie. "Once the carpet engines gain enough speed, the flaps point downward, causing lift. Thus, the so-called magic of flight."

"So, how does the Flying Carpet work as a carpet?"

"Shhh."

"The glue is what holds my horn in place," said the unicorn to the wide-eyed children.

"That doesn't explain how you can talk," queried Johnny.

"That's because I'm just a man in a horse costume," replied Frank.

"A house made entirely of candy?!?!?"

"There is no need to explain this. It is perfectly possible."

"The Queen uses a barbiturate cocktail to put her out," explained the medical technician to the Prince. "This IV drip kept her nourished, and then the steroid/adrenaline antidotal balm I secretly spread on your lips brought her out of the coma when you kissed her."

"What about the immortal possibilities of love?"

"As I've already said, it had more to do with the steroid/adrenaline balm."

"Half man, half bull!" said Jason. "You must be some sort of rare genetic anomaly!"

"No. I lost the top half of the bull costume," replied Frank.

"You're not a Beast at all."

"No. Just a metaphorical pariah."

"Throwing beans and chanting 'mamemaki' will clearly promote the chances that demons will avoid your house."

"What fairy tale is this?"

"It comes from the north of Japan."

"Well, maybe demons exist in Japan, but here they need to be explained."

TFTC Editor: So, you're saying if the conditions were just right, Jonah could survive in a whale's stomach?

Scientist: Please stop calling.

Seating Chart

by Kevin A. Doughten (2000)

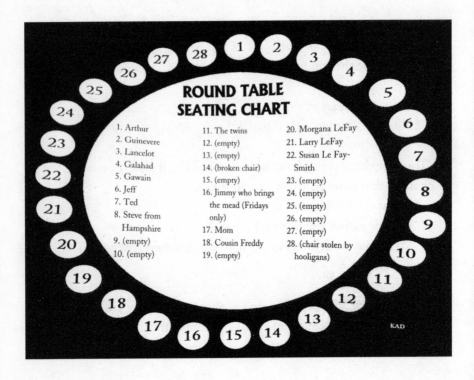

ROUND TABLE SEATING CHART

1. Arthur
2. Guinevere
3. Lancelot
4. Galahad
5. Gawain
6. Jeff
7. Ted
8. Steve from Hampshire
9. (empty)
10. (empty)
11. The twins
12. (empty)
13. (empty)
14. (broken chair)
15. (empty)
16. Jimmy who brings the mead (Fridays only)
17. Mom
18. Cousin Freddy
19. (empty)
20. Morgana LeFay
21. Larry LeFay
22. Susan Le Fay-Smith
23. (empty)
24. (empty)
25. (empty)
26. (empty)
27. (empty)
28. (chair stolen by hooligans)

KAD

Gag Gifts

by B. J. Novak (2001)

People love getting gag gifts—but what gag to give? This simple guide to gag gifts is the perfect gag gift for anyone who enjoys giving gag gifts without any outside guidance.

For a person who hates gag gifts:
    This one's too obvious—a gag gift! It works on two levels. This gag gift will be a jar of jelly beans that says "Sex Pills."

For a stand-up comedian:
    This guy makes a living off gags (and talking about gags), so a gag gift would just be something he could use professionally. Instead, slash his voice box. A silent comedian is a gag gift for the audience.

For a prisoner of war:
    "That joker! This is the only gift I don't need!" your friend would surely say about the gag you sent him—if he didn't already have an identical gag stuck in his mouth!

For a diabetic:
    A jar of sex pills. The label says "Jelly Beans."

For a prisoner of war contemplating suicide:
    Smuggle him a fake gun. When the trigger is pulled, out comes a flag that says POW! Not only will you avert the suicide, but you'll remind him of the state that drove him to attempt it. Gotcha!

For your wife:
    Formally revoke last year's gift (an official-looking piece of paper that says License to Be a Bitch). My mistake, honey.

For Dale Kupersmith, inventor of Viagra, the so-called sex pill:

A pen that gives you an electric shock. This is the ultimate gag gift.

Advice from a Car Thief

by Colin K. Jost (2003)

Unless you know exactly what you're doing, stealing a car can prove difficult and confusing. Here are a few guidelines to keep your head calm and your car stolen, presuming you now own someone else's car.

Don't steal cars from your own block and definitely don't steal cars from your own driveway. As a rule of thumb, don't steal anything from your own driveway—it's against the law.

Wear gloves to avoid leaving fingerprints, but never wear gloves with suction cups attached, unless the car is parked on the side of a building or on the side of another, more levitating car.

After you steal the car, don't speed away with the tires screeching. You'll only draw attention to yourself. Instead, remove the tires and walk the car home gently.

A great idea is to switch the stolen car's license plates with novelty plates that say Mine 4 Real.

Get your hands on a police radio. That way, when the cops are giving chase, you can trick them by pretending to be a policeman and saying, "I'll take it from here, pigs."

Might I suggest reverse psychology? Stereotypical thieves wear all-black outfits and sneak around at night. I staple Christmas lights to a neon-orange shirt and yell profanities while stealing fancy cars in broad daylight. Who would ever suspect I was a real thief? Apparently, several eyewitnesses, the police, a federal judge, and a jury of my peers.

Create a diversion like the sound of a wind of a sound-wind sounding a wind sounding SOUNDING WIND! (I just stole your car.)

Sketchy Situation

by Colin K. Jost and Rob Dubbin (2003)

Scene: A police station.

Victim: Police! Quick, I need a sketch artist. Someone just mugged me!

Jim, a sketch artist: I believe I can help you. What did this person look like?

Victim: There were two people actually—a man and a woman.

Jim: I see. Please describe the male.

Victim: Brown hair, blue eyes . . . a lot like me actually, but more muscular.

Jim: Hmmm. How does that look?

Victim: He was also naked. Huge dick.

Jim: That's odd. The woman?

Victim: A model. Nice breasts—two of them. And a *huge* vagina.

Jim: Did they attack you?

Victim: Sort of, but first they attacked each other by having sex.

Jim: Like this?

Victim: Still needs a bigger dick. Say . . . I'll get to keep this sketch, right?

Jim: Oh sure, no prob—wait a second! Are you just using me to get free porn?!

Victim: Are you just using *me* to get free audio erotica?

Jim: Point taken.

Bad Doctors

by Elizabeth S. Widdicombe (2006)

I love hearing the poors on TV complain about how health care is so terrible in this country. It reminds me of how, for a select few of us, the doctors are totally bribable.

Me: What's the story, doc?

Doctor: I'm sorry to tell you this, but you have type 3 tuberculosis.

Me: (*laughing*) Oh dear.

D: That's the incurable kind.

Me: (*waving a $1,000 bill*) Oh really? Is it really incurable?

D: Well, they're working on a—

Me: What about now? Are they still working on it? (*waving $100*)

D: No. It's curable.

Me: That's more like it. I'll have a cure, please. And you know what? Why don't you throw in some new boobs for the missus?

D: Certainly.

Me: Can your profession really make a man pregnant, like on the hilarious movie I saw?

D: I suppose we—

Me: (*waving $5*) Not me, of course. Just any man off the street will do.

D: Coming right up.

Me: And, Doctor?

D: Yes?

Me: It's my birthday.

D: Happy birthday, sir.

Me: Don't insult me. I want to see three strangers with my face.

Slumber Party

by Simon Rich (2006–2007)

Seymour: What do you guys want to do?

Zach: Let's find your dad's liquor and drink it!

Seymour: Cool! The only thing is: I don't know where the old man keeps his booze.

Dan: Well, let's split up and look for it! There are six of us. One of us is bound to find it.

Seymour: Awesome, let's do it!

(*Five minutes later.*)

Zach: I found it! It was in the first place I looked!

Dan: Really? I found one too.

Mike: Me too. Look.

Kevin: I . . . I also found some alcohol.

Seymour: Everyone found alcohol? I don't understand. Where did you guys look?

Zach: Under your dad's bed.

Dan: In your dad's medicine cabinet.

Josh: Behind your dad's toilet.

Kevin: A few different closets. And in your little sister's room . . . behind her community-service trophies.

Jake: I found a moonshine still in the basement. It looked pretty advanced. There were bags of barley and pressurized tanks. And there was some kind of silver tasting cup, hanging from a hook.

Seymour: I can't believe this. I think I have to be alone for a while.

Brent: (*running in*) Hey, Seymour! Guys! Guess what, I found the booze! You'll never guess where it was—in the attic inside an old box marked Memories.

Seymour: . . .

Brent: There was a lot up there.

Skydiving

by Robert I. Padnick (2007)

What's up, my name's Trad, and I'll be your skydiving instructor this afternoon. Now I know some of you may be scared, but you honestly have nothing to worry about. When you're in the plane, you'll have me—a very strong and powerful man—tightly strapped to your back, controlling your body and inching you step by step toward emptiness. Cool, breezy emptiness. And when you're in free fall, you'll be comforted as my lips caress your earlobe and softly whisper, "This is flying."

Now, I've got some strict rules. First, I never dive with a woman, not because it makes me uncomfortable, but because I fear that her breasts may attract condors. Second, I never dive strapped to a short person. The last time I tried that, his feet couldn't touch the ground when we landed, and to this day he still thinks he's plummeting. Third, you have to close your eyes when we fall through a cloud so as not to intrude on angels. Cool? So if you two women and you, short guy, could just hang out . . . feel free to grab a Dew.

Listen, you're all doing something great today. You're entering into skydiving history, from that first guy who looked at the sky and declared "That is something I want to be falling through" to the guy who saw the first airplane take flight and declared "It's about time." Maybe you'll be that first skydiver to realize that the parachute is just a crutch and that you can fly all on your own like Dumbo.

Finally, I would like to clear up the common misconception that it is somehow challenging to do flips and similar stunts while in the air. It's not. When you're surrounded by nothing but air for minutes, you can do as many flips as you want.

The Diary of Francisco Pizarro

by Benjamin U. Steiner (2009)

August 6—Land ho! We have nearly reached the New World, and the crew is positively giddy with anticipation and scarlet fever. With anticipation and more than the thrill of exploration is the prospect of meeting new friends along the way. We have all shaved our beards so as to appear nonthreatening.

August 9—I have stumbled upon a campground where natives are burning trees to the ground using our gunpowder. Is this some sort of spiritual offering? I plan to return tomorrow with my men so we can begin an open-minded discourse on the comparative merits of our two religions.

August 10—We returned to the campground today, but the natives refuse to enlighten us with their world view. Instead, all they do is bow to us and bring us gold. I keep telling them we just want to talk, but they won't stop chaining themselves together and performing menial labor long enough to listen. Whenever my men and I attempt to free them with our tools, they stubbornly insist that the only tools they need are the Bibles they have already stolen from us and memorized.

August 13—Our ship is so full of gold that it can barely stay afloat. I don't know when the natives transported it all, but they must have somehow done it while we were asleep. My only wish is that we had known ahead of time so we could have helped our generous new allies, or at least removed their shackles.

August 16—Now that they have no more gold to give us, the natives have taken to destroying their homes in frustration, and also building churches. My crew and I have no choice but to bathe in silent protest.

August 20—The natives keep running up to us, taking our weapons, and using those weapons to kill themselves before we have a chance to stop them. This has happened twelve thousand times.

Cosmopolitan June 2010
Editor's Page

by Chloe K. Goodwin (2011)

We would like to retract an assertion we made in our May 2010 article "The Top 100 Sexiest Places to Have Fun Summer Sex," #13—Ferris wheel car. This was an irresponsible and dangerous suggestion. Ferris wheels cars tend to oscillate to the extreme, and they go very high. Even the most adventurous Cosmogirl should not have sex in a Ferris wheel car.

The editors mourn the loss of *Cosmopolitan* subscriber Becky Friedman and guest.

A Cover from 2011

Cover by Jonathan P. Finn-Gamino

If I Were the Mayor

by Kevin P. Bartley (2011)

Illustration by Peter H. Manges

I wake up in a bathtub full of money. Twelve o'clock. Six of my wives come in the room and want to do sex to me. Can't, babes. I've got a lot of money to count today. And a lot of money to spend. Nobody ever said this mayor thing was going to be easy.

My servant shows me the newspaper headlines. MAYOR STILL AMAZING. It's good to know that the newspaper I control is on my side. Some people said I had a monopoly when I bought the entire town. Thank God the mayor never saw it that way.

I clock in. Someone has to run the town, and my next-door neighbor Cornwallis does a great job at that. He answers phone calls and delivers packages and sweeps floors—mayor stuff that I am too busy to do. When there's an important question, he runs it by the real man in charge. That guy is also a lifesaver.

Time for a meeting. My cabinet consists of the equally crucial positions of economic adviser and personal trainer. My economic adviser takes care of the town's financial problems, like when I run out of money or when I am so sick of money that we burn it to heat the homeless. The personal trainer doesn't help the town in any way. He's just a little perk that comes with the job.

I go outside and hear a guy screaming. I ask him what's wrong, and his jaw drops. It's the mayor. He tells me the courthouse is on fire and there are people trapped inside. What can be done? Open your car, I say. He does, and it is spectacular: candy beans of every flavor pour out and engulf him. "Mayor!" he cries. I leave the scene without ever telling him my name.

I walk on and hear a man say something about his son needing foot medicine. Coming right up. Can I get you anything else? A children's hospital? An orphanage? "There are no more orphans!" he cries. "You fed them all!"

Casanova

by Rob A. Knoll (2011)

—May I take this seat, m'lady?

—Oh, Casanova!

—I should say your gown is quite beautiful, but has not one half the craftsmanship of your radiant smile.

—Oh! Sir, you are— Did you drive here in that?

—Yes I did.

(*passionate lovemaking*)

—May I join you on your walk, madame?

—Heavens no! I've heard about you, Casanova, you vile, deceitful pig of a man!

—But nevertheless handsome, am I not?

—Everything about you is ugly.

—Even that car over there?

(*passionate lovemaking*)

—Beep-beep.

(*passionate lovemaking*)

—My lady, may I offer you a ride?

—Forgive me, sir, but I've been blind since childhood. Where are you?

—I'm sitting here. In my car.

—Oh, I hear you now. Thank you, I live just down the street.

—All right, uh . . . so can you tell what a car looks like by feeling it, like with faces?

—No, sir.

—Oh. Okay, we're here, I guess.

—Thank you, sir. Good-bye.

—Okay, bye.

—Hey, remember me?

—Your voice is familiar, but I fear I cannot see your face. I was stricken blind at a young—

—The car is red.

(*passionate lovemaking*)

Warren Buffett

by Jonathan D. Adler (2011)

W arren Buffett is a billionaire investor known for his thrifty
lifestyle. Unlike some of America's super-rich, who split their
time between homes in Palm Beach and Aspen, Buffett lives mod-
estly. This reporter journeyed to Buffett's home in Omaha, Nebraska,
to spend some time with America's favorite moneyed man.

Buffett, not a driver or assistant, picks me up from the airport
when I arrive. He drives a rust-stained 1989 Ford sedan. I tell
him the car makes sense for a man made famous by his long-term
investment strategies. "Nope. Just bought it this morning. I flipped
my other car, a Hyundai, for this one. Made a quick five." Thousand? "Just five." Buffett—drenched in billions—is not too big to
earn a buck wherever he can find it. "I left my briefcase in the other
car," he says. "It had our lunches in it."

As we pick our way through an Omaha Dumpster, Buffett speaks
about his foray into investing. "I had snuck into an office building in
hopes of finding a sink to bathe in," he recalls. "It turned out to be
a brokerage firm. When I was spotted, I confessed that I was tres-
passing. I had hoped for a night in jail—and the soup that comes
with it—but was instead offered a job."

We enter the public library, where Buffett stealthily tears pages
from books in the Young Adult section. "It's going to be freezing
tonight," he tells me as he stuffs paper into his shirt. He heads over
to the magazine section. Rather than reading the pretentious *Econ-
omist* or *Quarterly Journal of Economics*, he reaches for the local rag.
Famous for his attention to detail, Buffett eyes each page carefully
for market information, clipping retail coupons along the way. "It's
been six years since I've paid full price on a haircut," he says proudly.

From looking at him, you wouldn't know that his company just
completed a five-billion-dollar merger with a European plastics

company. The only merger Buffett wants to discuss is personal: "When I've got two pairs of pants that have just had it, I sew the good parts together to make one new pair." This explains his khakis/jeans, but not the adoration of his hometown. Everywhere we go, Buffett is greeted with cheers and salutations. As Buffett siphons gasoline from the car of an admiring local, I can't help but wonder how a man so wealthy can remain so normal. He is the everyman, and yet there is no one like him.

Most Likely to Succeed

by Ben H. Blatt (2013)

—Hey, Zach, I just voted you as Most Likely to Succeed for the senior superlatives.

—Really? I doubt I have a chance. I have a feeling LeBron James is going to win.

—You have a great shot. What's he good at other than basketball?

—They say he's going to be the first pick of the NBA draft. He'll be a millionaire next month.

—The star athlete is popular in high school, but where will he be ten years from now?

—I don't know if my talents are as obvious to everyone.

—I notice your talents. You're great with helping others and an awesome listener.

—That's exactly what Mrs. Weiss wrote in the comment section of my report card.

—You're a leader too. Remember when you started the wave at the state basketball championship?

—Yeah, people seemed to get into that. The kid sitting behind us gave me a pat on the shoulder after.

—A lot of people quietly admire you.

—Should I go tell Dan to vote for me? I may need a couple more supporters to put me over the edge.

—Dan will vote for you. I bet the entire debate team will vote for you.

—Should I start writing an acceptance speech? Do I get to give a speech if I win?

—I don't think so, but your name goes in the yearbook after the thirty-page basketball team section.

—My mother is going to be so happy.

—Look, there's LeBron now.

—Should I go shake his hand just so there won't be any hard feelings?

The Coup

by Katherine C. V. Damm (2013)

King: General, I overheard your men talking. Come speak with me.

General: My lord, I swear I have nothing to do with whatever you heard them plotting.

King: Don't play me for a fool. You thought I would be oblivious to a party being planned right under my nose!

General: Beg pardon?

King: The talk of sneaking to the castle, keeping it a secret from me or anyone loyal to the crown . . . I know what a surprise party is!

General: Oh! Certainly. A surprise party. You truly are a wise king to have uncovered this plot.

King: I know I am. But I am also a magnanimous king: I shall still act surprised.

General: I'm sure you will.

King: Is this an admirable surprise face?

General: Yes, sire, it is.

King: (*looking out window*) I see the peasants are coming! To think, I never thought they liked me very much.

General: It was their idea in the first place, my liege.

King: It seems they're bringing horses and spears. What is the theme of this party?

General: . . . Peasant themed.

King: Delightful. Will it be a potluck? Should I bring a boar?

General: Well, as you know, food has been very scarce for the past few months . . .

King: Oh, of course! Refreshments wouldn't make sense given the theme. I'll feast with my family beforehand. Are they invited?

General: Yes, everyone especially hopes your wife and firstborn son will attend.

King: Most certainly! Say nothing of this conversation, General. As king, it is my duty not to ruin the surprise.

Study Buddies

by Alexis C. Wilkinson (2015)

Dear Cynthia,

It is with a great heaviness in my heart and a :(on the screen of my TI-89 that I must inform you we can no longer be study buddies. I know this may come as a shock, which is why I have taken the time to write you this in-depth explanation and leave it in a place you are likely to find it, but without a return address or further method of contacting me.

I have chosen to terminate this study-buddy relationship not out of malice but out of genuine concern for our ability to be an effective team. You see, I work best when I can make a comprehensive study guide and review concepts well before a given assignment is due. You are a mountain gorilla. I do not know how best you work, but it is not conducive to my particular style.

Frankly, you possess a singular selfishness when it comes to sharing answers. I remember before the big final, when I generously gave you my complete study guide and you refused to even let me glimpse the corrected papers you had strewn to construct a nest in my stepmom's rumpus room. You are also strong. So very, very strong.

We are supposed to be friends and help each other on assignments. There is no *i* in *study buddies*. It really makes more of an *ee* sound. In *study buddies*, there is only *bud*. And *dies*, but this is unrelated.

I am sorry it had to end this way. See you in homeroom.

Sincerely,

Trish

Contributor Biographies

John Aboud III is a commentator on VH1 shows and a co-writer of *Penguins of Madagascar*.

Jonathan D. Adler has written for *The Tonight Show Starring Jimmy Fallon*.

Sarah J. Albee was a member of the *Lampoon*'s class of 1984.

Frederick L. Allen was an editor of *Harper's Weekly*.

Kurt B. Andersen is a novelist, radio host, and cofounder of *Spy* magazine.

Richard J. Appel has written for *The Simpsons* and served as executive producer and showrunner of *King of the Hill*, *American Dad*, *Family Guy*, and *The Cleveland Show*.

Elijah Aron is a writer and producer for *BoJack Horseman*.

Paul Bartlett was a member of the *Lampoon*'s class of 1902.

Kevin P. Bartley was a member of the *Lampoon*'s class of 2012.

Henry N. Beard is an author and cofounder of *National Lampoon*.

Alec H. Berg is an executive producer of *Silicon Valley* and has written for *Seinfeld*.

Hartwell Bishop was a member of the *Lampoon*'s class of 1903.

Ben H. Blatt is the coauthor of *I Don't Care if We Never Get Back* and a contributor to *Slate*.

Andy S. Borowitz was the creator of *The Fresh Prince of Bel-Air* and is a frequent contributor to *The New Yorker*.

Susan Stevenson Borowitz is a writer and was executive producer of *The Fresh Prince of Bel-Air*.

Walter R. Bowie, Jr., was a member of the *Lampoon*'s class of 1942.

John F. Bowman wrote for *Saturday Night Live*.

John D. Brancato wrote the screenplays for *Terminator 3: Rise of the Machines* and *The Game*.

Shirley Burden was a well-known photographer and writer.

J. Stewart Burns is a television writer and producer for *Unhappily Ever After*, *The Simpsons*, and *Futurama*.

Robert M. Carlock is the co-creator of *Unbreakable Kimmy Schmidt* and wrote for *30 Rock*.

Sidney Carroll was a screenwriter for films including *The Hustler* and *A Big Hand for the Little Lady*.

Daniel Chun has written for *The Office* and *The Simpsons*.

Kevin P. Curran wrote for *Late Night with David Letterman*.

Katherine C. V. Damm was a member of the *Lampoon*'s class of 2013.

Greg M. Daniels was the creator of *The Office*, *Parks and Recreation*, and *King of the Hill*.

Christopher L. Dingman was a member of the *Lampoon*'s class of 1986.

Kevin A. Doughten has written for *The New York Times*.

Jim Downey has written for *Saturday Night Live* and *Late Night with David Letterman*.

Mark A. Doyle was a member of the *Lampoon*'s class of 1982.

Mark J. Driscoll is a writer and producer for *Grey's Anatomy*, *Scandal*, and *Married with Children*.

Rob Dubbin has written for *The Late Show with Stephen Colbert* and *The Colbert Report*.

Thomas R. Feran, Jr., was a member of the *Lampoon*'s class of 1975.

Jonathan P. Finn-Gamino was a member of the *Lampoon*'s class of 2013.

Raymond A. Fitzgerald was a member of the *Lampoon*'s class of 1946.

Maya C. M. Forbes is the writer/director of *Infinitely Polar Bear*.

Ian A. Frazier is the author of *Great Plains* and a writer for *The New Yorker*.

Thomas W. Gammill has written for *Saturday Night Live*, *Seinfeld*, and *The Simpsons*.

Shannon C. Gaughan has written for *The Fresh Prince of Bel-Air* and *Saturday Night Live*.

John M. Gilpin was a member of the *Lampoon*'s class of 1973.

Chloe K. Goodwin was a member of the *Lampoon*'s class of 2012.

R. S. Gordon was an artist for the *Lampoon* in 1915.

Ted L. Greenberg has written for *Late Night with David Letterman*.

Lawrence M. Guterman is a director whose work includes *Cats & Dogs* and *Son of the Mask*.

Fred H. Gwynne starred in numerous films and television shows, including *The Munsters*, *Pet Sematary*, and *My Cousin Vinny*.

Ann H. Hodgman is a writer for *The New Yorker* and the author of several children's books and cookbooks.

Mel J. Horan was a member of the *Lampoon*'s class of 1979.

Walter S. Isaacson is a biographer and journalist and former managing editor of *Time*.

Al E. Jean wrote for *National Lampoon* and *The Simpsons*.

Colin K. Jost is a former head writer and "Weekend Update" co-anchor on *Saturday Night Live*.

Ken C. Keeler has written and produced for *Futurama* and *The Simpsons*.

Rob A. Knoll was a member of the *Lampoon*'s class of 2013.

Josh B. Lieb is a producer and showrunner of *The Tonight Show Starring Jimmy Fallon*.

Elizabeth M. Losh was a member of the *Lampoon*'s class of 1987.

David H. Mandel is an executive producer of *Veep* and *Curb Your Enthusiasm*.

Peter H. Manges was a member of the *Lampoon*'s class of 2015.

Patricia A. Marx, the first female member of *The Harvard Lampoon*, is a writer for *The New Yorker* and has also written for *Saturday Night Live*.

David C. K. McClelland was a cartoonist and writer for *National Lampoon, Harper's Magazine*, and *The New Yorker*.

Glenn P. McDonald was a member of the *Lampoon*'s class of 1989.

D. H. Mitchell wrote for the *Lampoon* in 1905.

Lewis Morton has written for *Saturday Night Live, Family Guy*, and *Futurama*.

Philip H. Muir was a member of the *Lampoon*'s class of 1905.

Pamela R. Norris wrote for *Saturday Night Live*.

B. J. Novak is an actor, writer, and producer best known for his work on *The Office*.

Justin A. Nowell was a member of the *Lampoon*'s class of 1998.

Conan C. O'Brien has hosted numerous late-night shows and written for *Saturday Night Live* and *The Simpsons*.

Stephen M. O'Donnell has written for *The Simpsons, Seinfeld*, and *Late Night with David Letterman*.

Mark P. O'Donnell wrote the Broadway shows *Hairspray* and *Cry-Baby.*

Dan J. O'Keefe is a writer and producer for *Silicon Valley.*

Samuel S. Otis was a notable architect.

David L. Owen is an author and writer for *The New Yorker.*

Robert I. Padnick has written for *Man Seeking Woman* and *The Office.*

Vincent Palmer was a member of the *Lampoon*'s class of 1935.

Roger Parloff is a senior editor at *Fortune* magazine.

Stuart A. Pizer was a member of the *Lampoon*'s class of 1966.

George A. Plimpton was a journalist and cofounder of *The Paris Review.*

Paul S. Redford is co-executive producer of *The Newsroom*, and was a writer and producer of *The West Wing.*

Mike L. Reiss is a showrunner, writer, and producer of *The Simpsons.*

Eugene Reynal was a member of the *Lampoon*'s class of 1924.

Simon Rich is a novelist, humorist, and writer for *Saturday Night Live, Man Seeking Woman,* and *The New Yorker.*

Adam E. Rosen was a member of the *Lampoon*'s class of 1995.

Francis W. Saunders was a member of the *Lampoon*'s class of 1925.

William W. Scott was a member of the *Lampoon*'s class of 1925.

Jonathan A. Shayne was a member of the *Lampoon*'s class of 1984.

Paul R. Simms has directed and produced *Flight of the Conchords* and written for *Girls*.

James D. Stanley was a member of the *Lampoon*'s class of 1959.

Benjamin U. Steiner was a member of the *Lampoon*'s class of 2011.

Nicholas A. Stoller has directed numerous films, including *Forgetting Sarah Marshall* and *Neighbors*.

Danny L. Tobey is the author of *The Faculty Club*.

George W. S. Trow, Jr., was an essayist and writer for *The New Yorker*.

W. Tuckerman wrote for the *Lampoon* in 1903.

John H. Updike was a novelist, essayist, and poet, most famous for his Rabbit series.

Patric M. Verrone has written for *Futurama* and *The Simpsons*.

Arthur W. Viner was a member of the *Lampoon*'s class of 1942.

Morgan D. Wheelock was a member of the *Lampoon*'s class of 1960.

Elizabeth S. Widdicombe is a writer for *The New Yorker*.

Alexis C. Wilkinson, the first black female president of *The Harvard Lampoon*, has written for *Veep* and *Brooklyn Nine-Nine*.

Gluyas Williams was a celebrated cartoonist for *The New Yorker*.

Maiya M. Williams, the first black officer of *The Harvard Lampoon*, has written for *The Fresh Prince of Bel-Air, Mad TV,* and *Futurama*.

Steve E. Young has written for *Late Night with David Letterman*.

John P. Ziaukas has written for *Unhappily Ever After*.

The *Harvard Lampoon* is an ancient humor magazine based in Cambridge, Massachusetts. Its historic building, known as the Castle, is crawling with comedy and also, usually, cockroaches. Each year, the *Lampoon* publishes five issues and a small compendium of fables.